Copyright © 1992, 1995 Omnibus Press (A Division of Book Sales Limited)

Editorial by Suzi Black, Chris Charlesworth & Kalen Rogers
Cover & Book designed by 4i limited & Amy MacIntyre
Photo research by David Brolan & Amy MacIntyre

US ISBN 0.8256.1539.9   UK ISBN 0.7119.5424.0   Order No. OP 47808

All rights reserved. No part of this book may be reproduced in any form or by any electronic or mechanical means, including information storage or retrieval systems, without permission in writing from the publisher, except by a reviewer who may quote brief passages.

Exclusive distributors:
BOOK SALES LIMITED
8/9 Frith Street, London W1V 5TZ, UK.

MUSIC SALES CORPORATION
257 Park Avenue South, New York, NY 10010, USA.

MUSIC SALES PTY LTD.
120 Rothschild Avenue, Rosebery, NSW 2018, Australia.

To the Music Trade only:
MUSIC SALES LIMITED
8/9 Frith Street, London W1V 5TZ, UK.

Photo Credits:
David Anderson/SIN, A.J. Barratt/Retna, Edie Baskin/Retna, Richard Bellia, Jay Blakesberg/Retna, Bourquaro/Stills/Retna, George Chin, Jeff Davy/Retna, Steve Double/Retna, Steven Freeman/Retna, Steve Granitz/Retna, Steve Guillick/Retna, Charles Hoselton/Retna, Mick Hutson/Retna, A. Indge/Retna, Ian Lawson/SIN, Youri Lenquette/Stills/Retna, Levy/Stills/Retna, Michel Linssen/Retna, London Features International, Tony Mottram/Retna, Peter Orth/Retna, Charles Peterson/Retna, Michela Petroni/SIN, Doralba Picerno/SIN, David Redfern/Retna, Relay Photos, Ed Sirrs/Retna, Steven Sweet/Retna, Justin Thomas/Retna, Ian T. Tilton/Retna, Ian T. Tilton/SIN, Scott Weiner/Retna, Alice Wheeler/Retna.

Front cover photograph: Levi Philippe/Retna
Back cover: Charles Peterson/Retna

Printed in the United States of America by Vicks Lithograph and Printing Corp.

OMNIBUS PRESS

NIRVANA

Isn't it strange how some people never learn? "Would you let your daughter marry a Rolling Stone?", sneered one of Britain's respected daily rags when Jagger, Richard, Jones, Wyman and Watts emerged from the Dartford delta with a raunchy brand of Chicago R&B, and hair that flapped dangerously over their shirt collars. It began as a joke, but those of a certain age and beyond continued to speculate about what kind of people would wear their hair that long, and pull those faces, and anyway, did they ever wash? And what kind of morals were buzzing around those hair-drenched heads of theirs?

> "I LIKED ANYTHING THAT WAS A LITTLE BIT WEIRD, A LITTLE BIT DIFFERENT. I ALWAYS WENT FOR THE PSYCHOTIC, WEIRD, 'DIRGEY' BANDS."
> **KURT**

When The Rolling Stones toured America for the first time in the late summer of 1964, worse was to come. They were fine on the East and West coasts, which had already lived through the beatniks and the bohemians and discovered that life in the aftermath went on pretty much the same. In the South and the great Mid-West, though, no-one came to their shows; no self-respecting redneck boy or girl would want to be seen dead at a gathering of tribes like that.

It took one American institution to stand up for another. Veteran comedian, singer, actor, Sinatra hanger-on and famed imbiber Dean Martin talked himself into rock history when he championed the American dream of free speech live on TV in front of an audience of millions — and a ready-assembled bunch of victims called The Rolling Stones. Public demand entailed the Stones appearing on his show, but Dean wasn't letting them off that easily. He sent out withering jabs of supposed wit in their direction, questioning their gender, suggesting they might profitably be dragged to a barber, and alleging that the dirt lay inch-thick around their skulls. For his sins, he won a cheap laugh, and the undying contempt of everyone who's heard the story since.

Fast forward nearly three decades. The scene is a cramped television studio in London, where a small group of teenagers are being herded forcibly from one camera angle to the next in a desperate attempt to simulate excitement for the viewing public. The programme, of course, is Top Of The Pops, the BBC's weekly half-hour indulgence of young people and their music. Little more than a joke for generations of intelligent music fans, Top Of The Pops is still necessary viewing, as it is occasionally dragged out of its comfortable middle-of-the-road stance by a chart interloper with revolutionary intentions.

So it is that early in 1992, the programme airs a video featuring Nirvana, unquestionably the hottest rock band in the world. It fades early — nothing on pop television dare last longer than two minutes — revealing a dapper DJ in full dance-club regalia. It's his job to name the records, and make the whole deal sound exciting. Instead, he sneers the name of the band at his audience, and adds a throw-away tag-line: "They could do with a good clean-up, couldn't they?" And then we're off on something really exciting, another production-line dance ditty that's all synthesized rhythm and no soul.

By setting himself up for all that's sanitised and safe, and against long hair, loud guitars and burning passion, the anonymous DJ has fulfilled his role in the illustrious history of television's crusade against the bizarre, the revolutionary, the meaningful, the real. He's right there alongside Dean Martin and his ilk, confident that by bad mouthing what he doesn't like, he can make it go away — not realising that by cheapening himself with a slick jibe at Nirvana, he's simply solidified the loyalty of their fans, and pushed another layer of the uncommitted off the fence and onto the battleground. When they're scared enough to come up with lines like that, you can tell they know they're losing.

> "WE'RE SO TRENDY THAT WE CAN'T EVEN ESCAPE OURSELVES."
> **KURT**

'Like Long Hair' was a war cry thirty years earlier, when Paul Revere and The Raiders came out of America's North-West corner as the commercial wing of one of rock's least recognised movements. For several years in the early Sixties, Seattle and Washington were the core of a punk-rock uprising, as

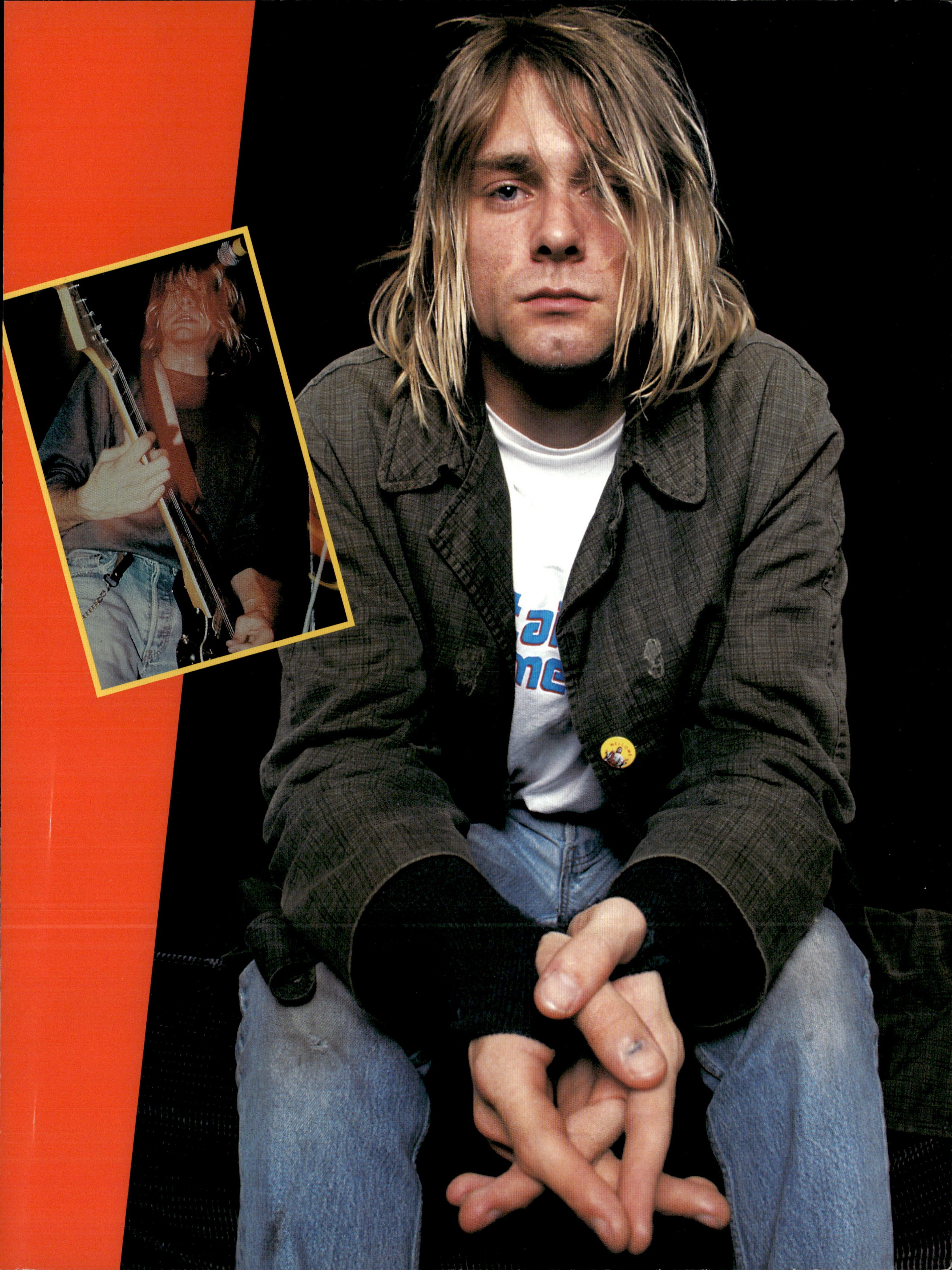

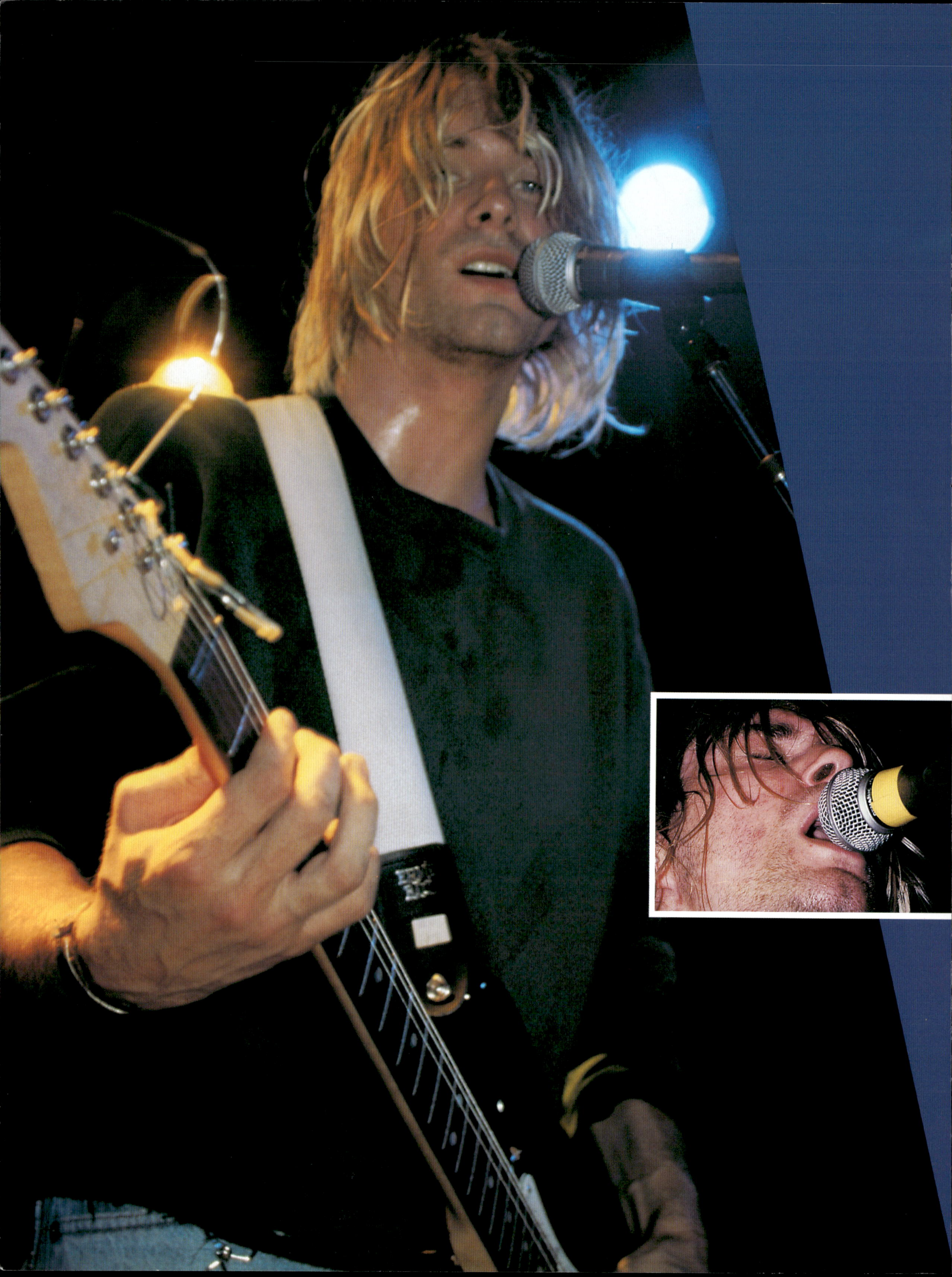

bands like The Kingsmen, The Sonics, The Raiders and The Wailers took the three-chord tradition of rock'n'roll, added the instrumental raunch of Duane Eddy and Link Wray, and emerged with a fearsome brand of garage rock that was a beacon of fire in the midst of an anodyne era in American popular music.

"I DON'T WANT TO BE ASSOCIATED WITH NINETY-NINE PER CENT OF ALL ROCK AND ROLL BANDS."
KURT

In the Sixties, these local explosions could pass almost unnoticed. A single or two would cross over to the national charts, but without prime-time TV exposure, home-state stars could be unknown across the county line. In the Nineties, we have MTV, a religion among American teens and twenties. Cable television has converted the mass of young Americans to such idiosyncratic performers as Prince, Run-DMC and Guns N'Roses. Now it's made superstars and role models out of a trio of North-Western hardcore rockers called Nirvana — whose blistering instrumental attack, sly melodic skill and bleak lyrical angst have combined to make them the most interesting, and biggest-selling, rock band in America.

A statistical interlude demonstrates their impact. Their record label pressed up a modest 50,000 copies of their last album in September 1991; within four months, they'd been forced to run off more than two million. Some 70,000 people a day were entering their local store and requesting the record in question, Nevermind. With only a low promotional budget invested in their charges, Geffen Records suddenly found themselves with the No. 1 record in the country — outselling albums by Michael Jackson, U2, Dire Straits and Guns N'Roses which had been hyped as historical events, and exposed as damp squibs.

The record industry measures success in figures, and on that tally alone, Nirvana might easily be another Bon Jovi, or Def Leppard, or Aerosmith: hard rock sugar-candy for the masses, all swagger and no surprise, carefully concocted and crafted down to the last scripted pout and pose in front of the ever-present TV camera.

One listen to the music cuts through that possibility. Nirvana's sound is bleak, uncompromising, eerie, challenging, thrilling, terrifying — everything that rock'n'roll was always supposed to be. In a Western world where capitalism has produced the twin pinnacles of poverty and excess, and where every fresh taste seems to have been calculated by the marketing men before it reaches your mouth, there's something exhilarating about a band who have the daring to question the machine which has created their success, and who wonder whether fame is going to prove fatal more than obscurity.

"WE'RE JUST A BAR BAND, THAT'S ALL WE ARE."
KURT

Cultural commentators point to a growing realisation amongst American and British youth that materialism is, at root bottom, empty. But its bloodsucking tentacles have squeezed out the last vestiges of the brave, naïve idealism which kept the children of the Sixties from the nihilism of today.

In Nirvana, two million listeners and more have found a voice for their doubts and fears. Nirvana don't offer any answers; these days, it's an achievement to pose the questions. If they have any message for the world, it extends to three words: think for yourself. No wonder the music industry, from the millionaire record company bosses to that Top Of The Pops DJ, thinks they're subversive.

Kurdt Kobain — or Kurt Cobain, or Kurdt Cobain, depending which record sleeve you read and believe — was born at the height of the flower power era in one of the few areas of America not to fall prey to the psychedelic explosion. Fly to Seattle, Washington, the North-Western-most city in the United States, one hundred miles short of the Canadian border. Take Interstate 405 out of the city, resist the temptation when you reach Olympia to plunge South towards California, and swing West instead on Highway 12 towards the Pacific Ocean. Just before you reach the end of the world, you'll find Aberdeen, concisely described by Cobain as "Twin Peaks without the excitement". Aberdeen was, and still is, a one-industry town; and that industry is logging, which is physical enough to sort out the men from the boys and make sure that the men are tough, uncompromising and none too happy about anything resembling a rebel.

"WE THOUGHT WE'D SELL A COUPLE OF HUNDRED THOUSAND RECORDS AT THE MOST, AND THAT WOULD BE FINE. THE NEXT THING YOU KNOW, WE GO TOP TEN."
KURT

"Aberdeen was nothing but rednecks and guns and booze," Cobain noted after his escape, "totally secluded from any culture at all". That's where he was raised, the son of a machinist — part of a happy family until 1976, when Cobain was around nine, and his parents decided to separate. Kurt spent the best part of two years sharing a trailer with his father, before opting to return home to his mother in 1978.

Like all towns centred around one industry, Aberdeen was subject to the roller-coaster ride of the international finance market. Feeling that their destiny was always out of their hands, the men of the town were prone to violence and depression. Shootings were commonplace, with the gunmen more often turning their barrels on themselves than outsiders; and those who didn't commit suicide kept themselves alive on drink, and a shared love of physical activity and sports.

For a sensitive, artistic child like Kurt, struggling to deal with the aftermath of his parents' separation, the town might as well have been renamed Hell. Cobain grew up to hate the macho ethos of the male community, and in turn it distrusted him. "All the other kids just wanted to fight and get laid," Cobain recalled, and though he

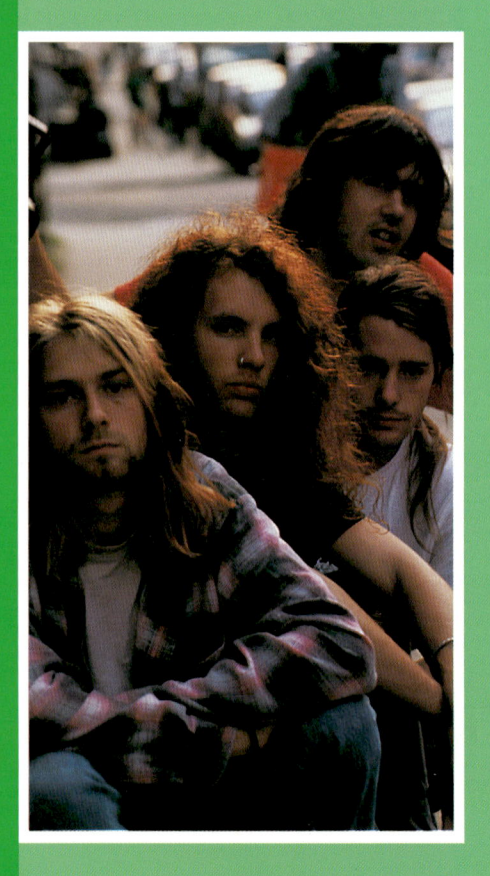

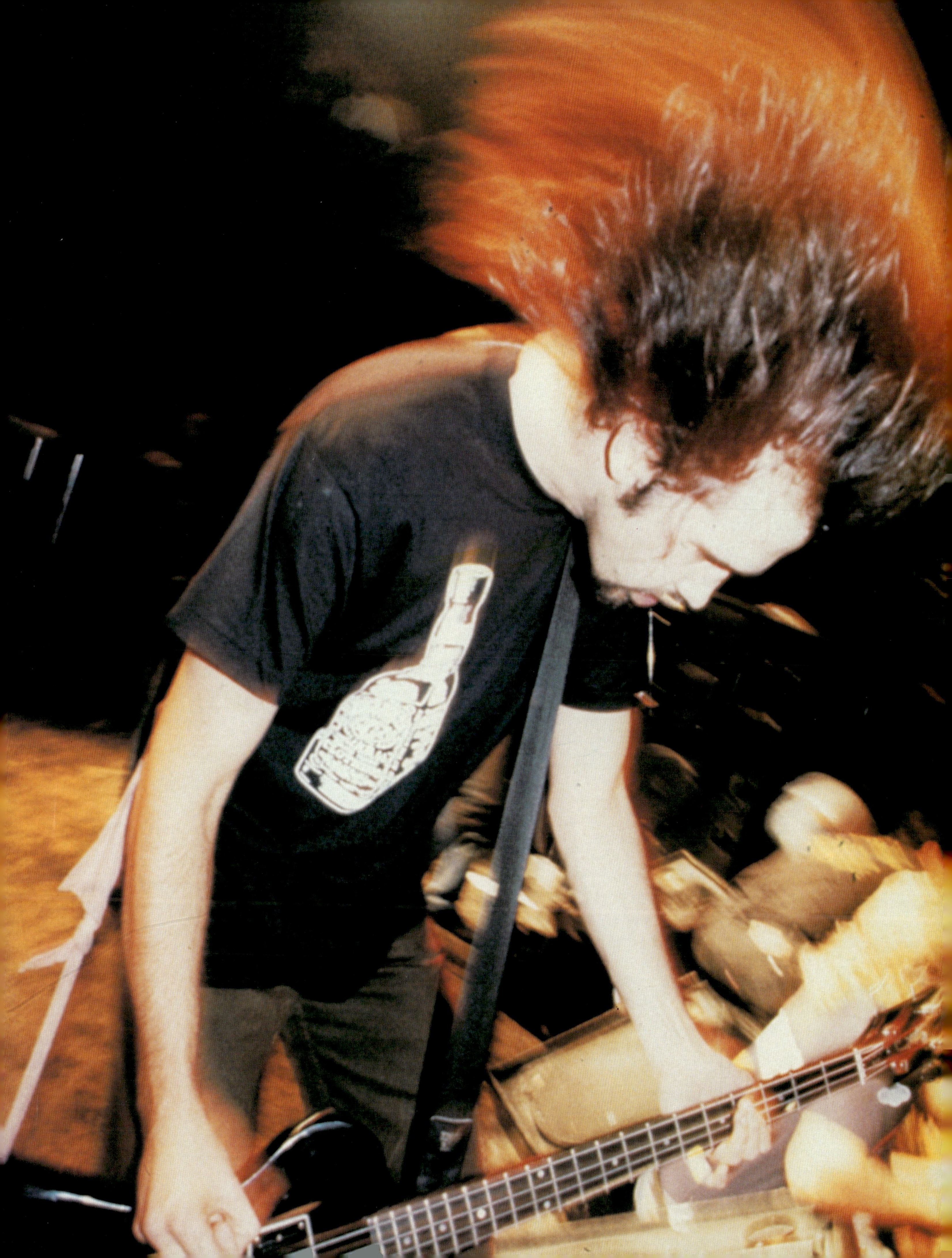

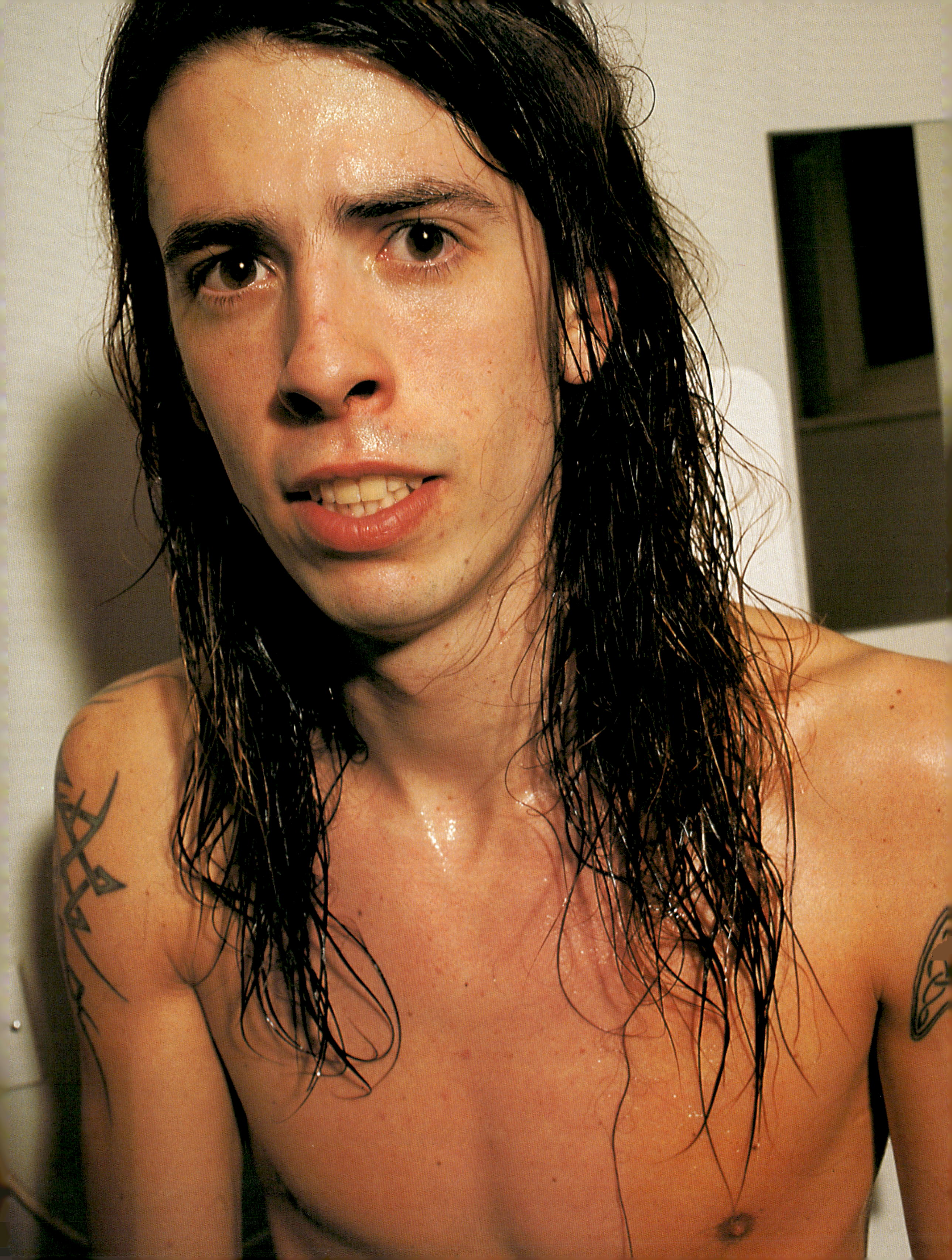

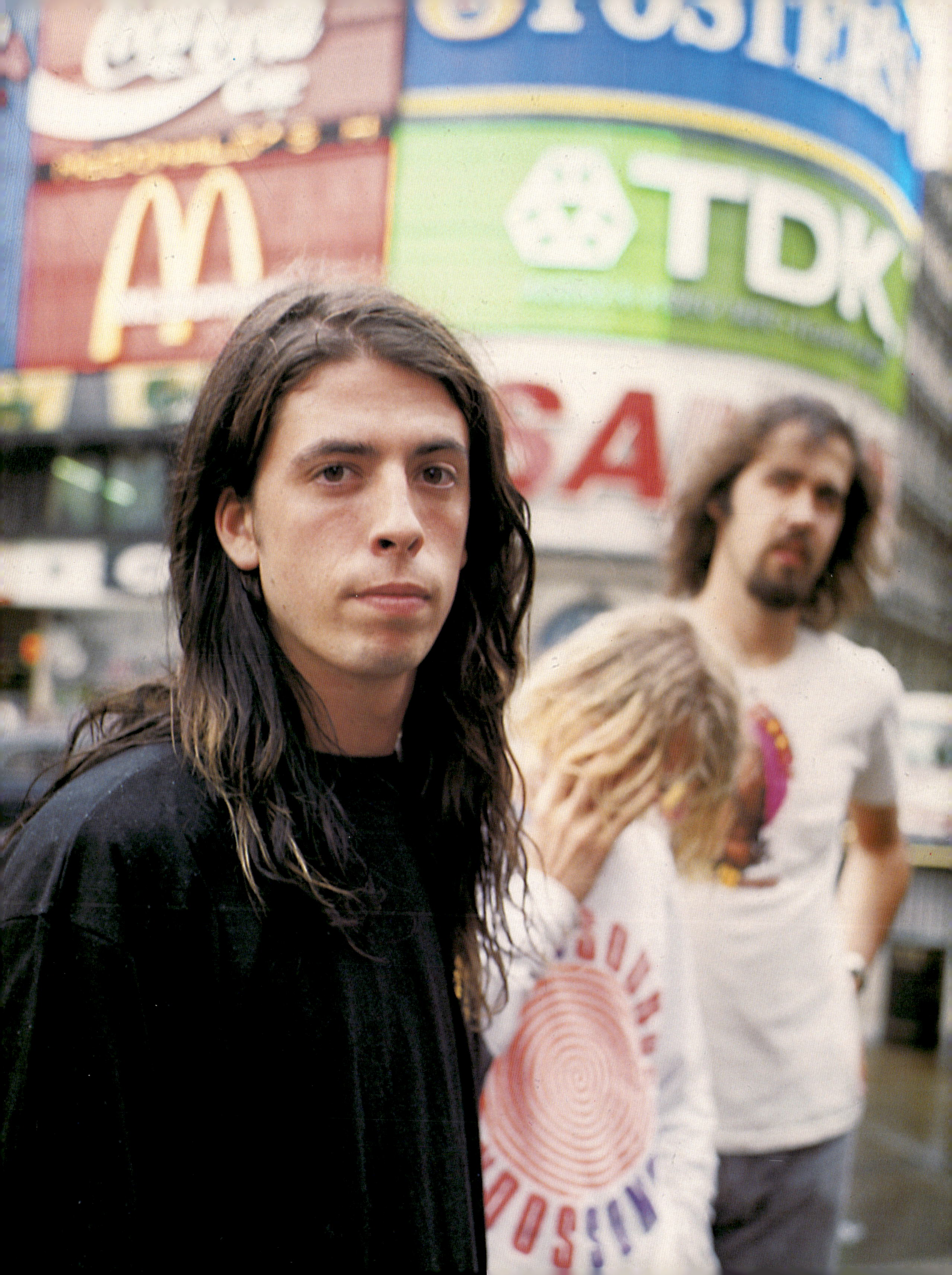
TDK

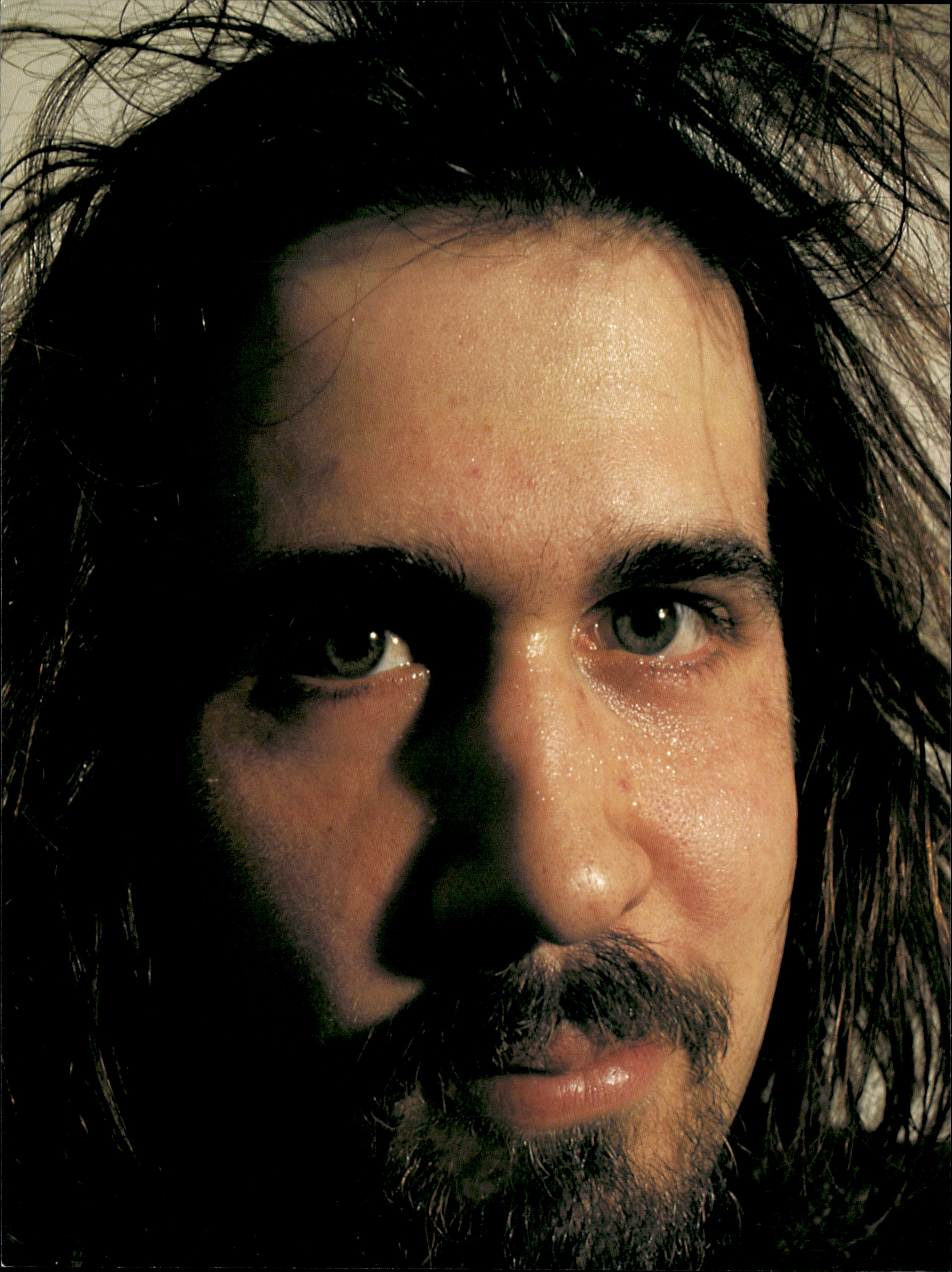

could see the attractions, he had deeper needs that Aberdeen couldn't satisfy. By his teens, he had begun to seek solace in petty crime — breaking and entering, not to steal, but purely for the sake of crossing forbidden boundaries; vandalism; generally unsocial behaviour. The story goes that he was arrested three times in his mid-teens; if he'd stayed, Cobain might have become another Aberdeen casualty.

> "WE BREAK THINGS ALL THE TIME, BUT THAT'S JUST US COMPENSATING FOR THE FRUSTRATION OF BEING ON THE ROAD."
> — KURT

His escape route, as it had been for as long as he could remember, was music. Born around the time that The Beatles' Sgt. Pepper album was released, Cobain was ideally placed to become a Beatlemaniac. "I wanted to be John Lennon," he admitted later. "I listened to The Beatles' records every night, religiously." He daydreamed by imagining what it would be like when The Beatles played in Aberdeen; it wasn't until 1976 that he learned the Fab Four had split up six years earlier.

Through his father, Kurt had also been exposed to heavy metal bands like Led Zeppelin and Black Sabbath. At the age of 11, while pursuing news of his heroes in the pages of Creem, Cobain was introduced to the concept, if not yet the sound, of punk. By his own admission, he tracked The Sex Pistols through the apocalyptic final tour of America with the fervour of a saint, entranced by their clothes, their hair, their attitude. "Punk changed my whole attitude to music," he said later. "What I wanted to do was play rhythm guitar in a band." Without access to records by The Pistols or The Clash, though, all he could do was imagine what punk sounded like. Not until 1981 did he hear one of the punk pioneers for the first time, when his local record library finally invested in a copy of The Clash's Sandinista!. Rushing the package home, Cobain discovered to his disgust that The Clash were now playing at being a reggae band. This wasn't the sound which had fuelled his fantasies: he returned to the music he shared with his peers, Iron Maiden and AC/DC.

> "RAPE IS ONE OF THE MOST TERRIBLE CRIMES ON EARTH. THE PROBLEM WITH GROUPS WHO DEAL WITH RAPE IS THAT THEY TRY TO EDUCATE WOMEN ABOUT HOW TO DEFEND THEMSELVES. WHAT REALLY NEEDS TO BE DONE IS TO TEACH MEN NOT TO RAPE, TO GO TO THE SOURCE AND START THERE."
> — KURT

The year of change was 1983, when Cobain was sixteen. It was then that he was first exposed to America's own mutation of English punk-rock, in the form of Black Flag and Scratch Acid — aggressive, raging, nihilistic music, which lashed out at political and social oppression without seeing hope in anything but decay and self-destruction. Cobain had found a handful of like-minded teenagers amidst Aberdeen's wastelands, and gradually he was introduced to bands like The Stooges, whose death-metal was the inspiration for the contemporary punk outfits.

The following year, Kurt left home, abandoning the orderliness of his mother's house for the danger and occasional excitement of bumming with friends, or in cars. Though his condition had not yet been diagnosed, he had begun to show signs of narcolepsy, an incomprehensible illness which strikes its victims asleep as they stand. Working for a few weeks as a hotel janitor, Cobain spent more hours asleep in unoccupied rooms than he did in the menial sweeping and cleaning which was supposed to be his vocation. That wasn't his only job in his late teens; in 1985, he worked briefly as a lifeguard at the local YMCA. But nothing lasted for long — except music.

That year, Cobain made the fateful connection, when he met the 19-year-old Chris Novoselic. Born in Los Angeles into a family of Yugoslavian extraction, Novoselic was brought to Aberdeen before he reached his teens as his father entered the logging industry. He was a confirmed fan of unlikely bedfellows Led Zeppelin and Devo, but shared two things in common with Cobain — a friendship with Buzz Osbourne, who was the singer with a Seattle band called The Melvins, and a passionate desire to create music of his own.

> "I DEFINITELY HAVE A PROBLEM WITH THE AVERAGE MACHO MAN, BECAUSE THEY HAVE ALWAYS BEEN A THREAT TO ME. I'VE HAD TO DEAL WITH THEM MOST OF MY LIFE — BEING TAUNTED AND BEATEN UP BY THEM IN SCHOOL. I DEFINITELY FEEL CLOSER TO THE FEMININE SIDE OF THE HUMAN BEING THAN I DO TO THE MALE."
> **KURT**

Without ever coming close to commercial acceptance, The Melvins were acknowledged as the centre of the Seattle underground rock scene. Dragged away from the rest of the American continent by the geographical enclosures of water (the Puget Sound and the Columbia River) and mountains (foremost among them the volcanic Mount St. Helens), the North-West of Washington State evolved at a different pace and angle to the rest of the USA. That same sense of isolation which left its more perceptive inhabitants feeling culturally bereft allowed the area's rock scene to develop a sound and style of its own.

So was born the hardcore punk sound that eventually swept its way across the nation. Buzz Osbourne, Dave Crover and Matt Lukin formed The Melvins at the start of the decade, and their Gluey Porch Treatments on the Alchemy label epitomised the ferocious, uncompromising attitude of the movement. At the same time, bands like Mr Epp, the Limp Richards and The Ducky Boys were appearing on the scene — none of them destined to survive for long, but each a vital ingredient in forming the sound of Seattle.

The unofficial Bible of the Seattle underground was Bruce Pavitt's fanzine Subterranean Pop, which first appeared in 1979 and became Sub Pop the following year. As early as 1981, Pavitt was compiling cassettes of the city's undiscovered talent, with the long-term aim of launching a record label that would capture the region's identity on wax.

> "I'M A SPOKESMAN FOR MYSELF. IT JUST SO HAPPENS THAT THERE ARE A BUNCH OF PEOPLE THAT ARE CONCERNED WITH WHAT I SAY. I FIND THAT FRIGHTENING AT TIMES, BECAUSE I'M AS CONFUSED AS MOST PEOPLE. I DON'T HAVE THE ANSWERS FOR ANYTHING. I DON'T WANT TO BE A FUCKING SPOKESPERSON."
> **KURT**

The fanzine disappeared after 1983, but Pavitt continued to be a prime mover on the Seattle scene. Eventually, in 1986, he achieved his dream, inaugurating the Sub Pop label with the financial backing of local entrepreneur and aspiring musician, Jonathan Poneman. Pavitt and Poneman devoted more and more energy to the label,

NIRVANA

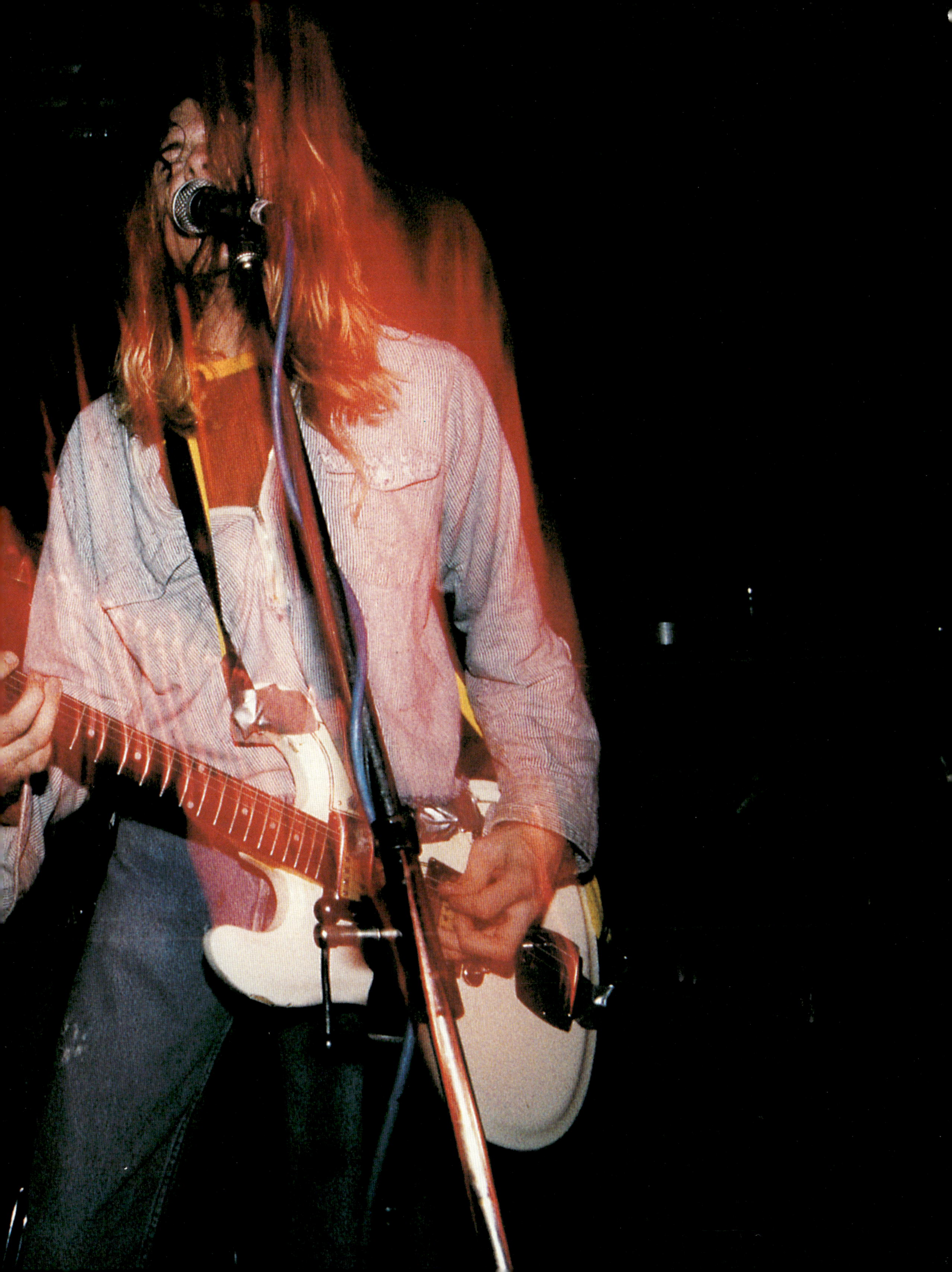

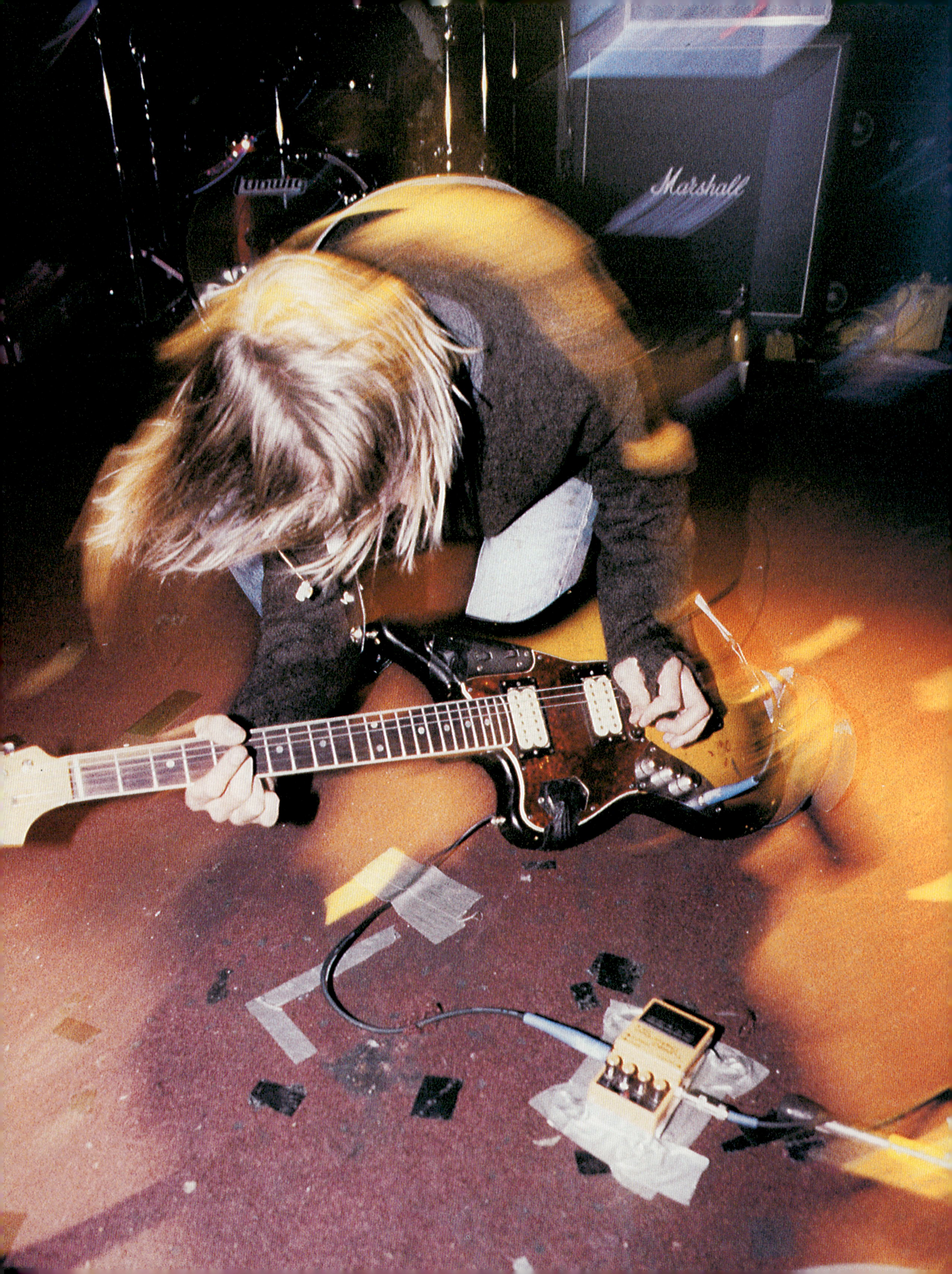
Marshall

and within two years it was being recognised internationally as America's most promising hotbed of new talent.

The first Sub Pop release, a compilation called Subpop 100, looked beyond the state boundaries for its kicks, taking in contributions from Sonic Youth and Skinny Puppy as well as less familiar bands. Thereafter, the focus switched closer to home. Pavitt and Poneman spent the best part of a year investigating the local talent, and then spotlighted two vital bands in Seattle's evolution, Green River and Soundgarden. From the start, Sub Pop aimed itself at collectors, striking a firm label identity with its limited edition, coloured vinyl singles. The aim was to make its patrons feel they belonged to an élite, an impression reinforced when Pavitt and Poneman formed the Sub Pop Singles Club in 1988.

For the moment, Green River and Soundgarden dominated the early release sheets, alongside lesser outfits like Swallow and Fluid. Green River was a synthesis of two earlier bands, Mr Epp and Spluii Numa: formed in 1984, they ultimately split three years later, dividing amoeba-like into two significant Seattle bands, Mudhoney and Mother Love Bone. And in time, Mother Love Bone would also disintegrate and be reborn as Pearl Jam. Such was the incestuous nature of the Seattle scene, however, that members crossed ranks and guested with each other in the studio and in performance at liberty — until the more stringent restrictions of international recording contracts intervened at the end of the decade.

"I'M A NARCOLEPTIC, SO I HAVE A HARD TIME BEING MOTIVATED. I FORGET THINGS ALL THE TIME."
KURT

Back in Aberdeen, Kurt Cobain and Chris Novoselic were some way short of being ready to audition for Sub Pop. In 1985, the duo made some initial demos with Dave Crover, under the name Fecal Matter; they formed a band concentrating on the Creedence Clearwater Revival back

VANDALIS
BEAUTIFUL AS
IN A COP'S F

CA THE FEVER

CA THE FEVER

CA THE FEVER

catalogue; they discovered the joys of acid; they were branded satanists by their appalled neighbours; and they borrowed a four-track recorder from Cobain's aunt. With a drummer called Aaron Burkhart, they moved beyond the Aberdeen city limits to experiment with gigs in Olympia, and then thirty miles further up the Sound to Takoma. From there, it was an hour's drive to Seattle, where they moved in 1986. "That was our big goal," Cobain recalls: having achieved it, they took the memorable decision to name their band Nirvana, after the shared Buddhist and Hindu concept of release from the endless cycle of reincarnation. In nirvana, all earthly desires are fulfilled and extinguished: human existence comes to an end, and the fortunate subject reaches a state of absolute blessedness. The choice of name was, you can be sure, ironic. Aaron Burkhart having vanished along the way, and two other contenders surviving no more than a matter of weeks, Chad Channing became Nirvana drummer No. 4. For the next two years, the band remained in Seattle, sharing concert bills with the likes of Mudhoney and Beat Happening, burning the true flame of punk-rock with few frills or concession to accessibility, and gradually excising unnecessary complications from their music. "We were very afraid to play pop music," Cobain noted later, "because we felt that most people wouldn't accept it."

> "PEOPLE JUST DON'T DO THINGS VERY OFTEN ANYMORE. I'M KIND OF DISTURBED BY IT."
> **KURT**

It was a period of quiet consolidation for Nirvana and the rest of the Seattle scene. While 1987 passed with a flurry of personnel crises across the hardcore circuit, few records came out of the chaos. In 1988, though, Sub Pop caught its stride, and soon singles were emerging from Pavitt and Poneman's operation every month. Nirvana watched as their friends and contemporaries in bands like Tad and Mudhoney were gathered under Sub Pop's wing: finally, towards the end of the year, Cobain, Novoselic and Channing were invited to make their first record for the label.

Nirvana's début was, happily enough, also the début of the Sub Pop Singles Club. Restricted to 1,000 numbered copies, their 'Love Buzz'/'Big Cheese' single was released, and quickly sold out, in October 1988. The Singles Club concept encouraged the unusual, with bands like Mudhoney and Sonic Youth recording each other's material on the same single. So Nirvana didn't feel out of place by volunteering a cover of 'Love Buzz', a vintage song by the Dutch hitmakers of 'Venus', Shocking Blue. By comparison with their later work, 'Love Buzz' was restrained and surprisingly commercial, building on a quirky bass line and a thudding backbeat with a roar of guitars. Cobain's vocals sneered, then screamed, and the Nirvana sound took hold, with a rush of feedback and the first hints of the delirium — that uncanny sense of a mind losing control — that underpins all their best work. The flipside of the single was Cobain's 'Big Cheese', which epitomised the band's basic approach with its mix of melody and mayhem. Without shaking the city's foundations, Nirvana had announced their arrival in no uncertain terms.

Almost immediately, they began work on an album, which emerged under the title 'Bleach' in June 1989. "We recorded it in three days for $600 on eight tracks — we hacked it out," admitted Cobain. One song, 'Spank Thru', was premiered on another seminal label sampler, Sub Pop 200, at the end of 1988: like the album, it documented the full Nirvana experience.

> "I'M SURE ONCE GUNS N' ROSES GOT AS BIG AS THEY DID, THE GOVERNMENT CHECKED UP ON IT AND REALISED THEY DIDN'T HAVE THE BRAINS TO BE A THREAT TO ANYONE."
> **KURT**

The LP ranged from the Beatlesque 'About A Girl', which could have been written in 1964, to the screaming rant 'Negative

'Creep', a glimpse into the mind of a paedophile. Cobain's cynical view of the battle of the sexes was also aired on 'Swap Meet', while 'Floyd The Barber' slashed out at the small-town mentality of Aberdeen. While 'Downer', the theme song for the whole album, unveiled the band's love of punk, a more dominant influence was Black Sabbath — whose doomy, riff-laden early albums had long fallen out of critical favour, but had nonetheless fuelled the fantasies of more than one Seattle rocker.

At the heart of the album was an almost incoherent rage, which carried over to their live shows. While rivals like Mudhoney created a terrifying barrage of sound, it was still only music. With Nirvana, every menacing riff threatened to bring on the depression and claustrophobia of a migraine headache.

By the time the album was completed, Nirvana had auditioned and enlisted a second guitarist, Jason Everman — whose name appeared in the LP credits, though he had no involvement in making the record. Despite the favourable press response to 'Bleach', though, Nirvana were still a few million dollars away from superstardom. They lined up alongside the rest of the hopefuls on the Sub Pop roster at a series of showcases on the West Coast that spring and summer, and then in August they visited Britain for the first time, supporting Tad for between £50 and £100 a gig. Three months later they were back on these shores, playing third fiddle to Mudhoney as well as Tad at the elegantly titled Lame Festival at the Astoria in Charing Cross Road. Melody Maker had already begun to champion the band; this gave the rest of the British rock press a chance to catch up, and it was generally agreed that Nirvana stole the show.

"NOTHING IS BETTER THAN PLAYING LIVE, EVEN THOUGH WE MAY SAY WE HATE IT AND HAVE SAID WE MAY NOT CONTINUE TO PLAY LIVE. BUT PLAYING IN FRONT OF A BUNCH OF PEOPLE WHO REACT WELL IS THE BEST THING IN THE WORLD."
KURT

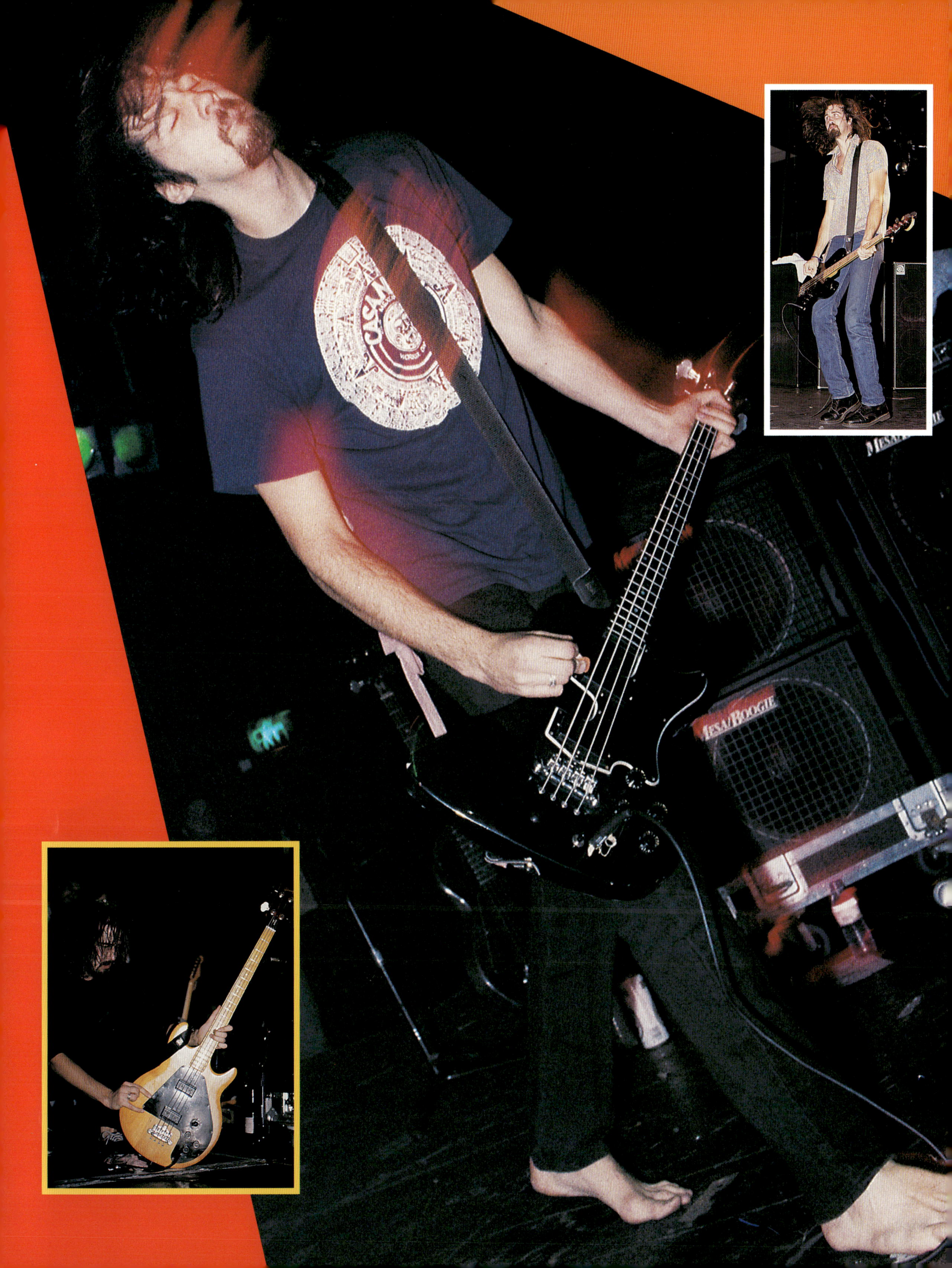
MESA/BOOGIE

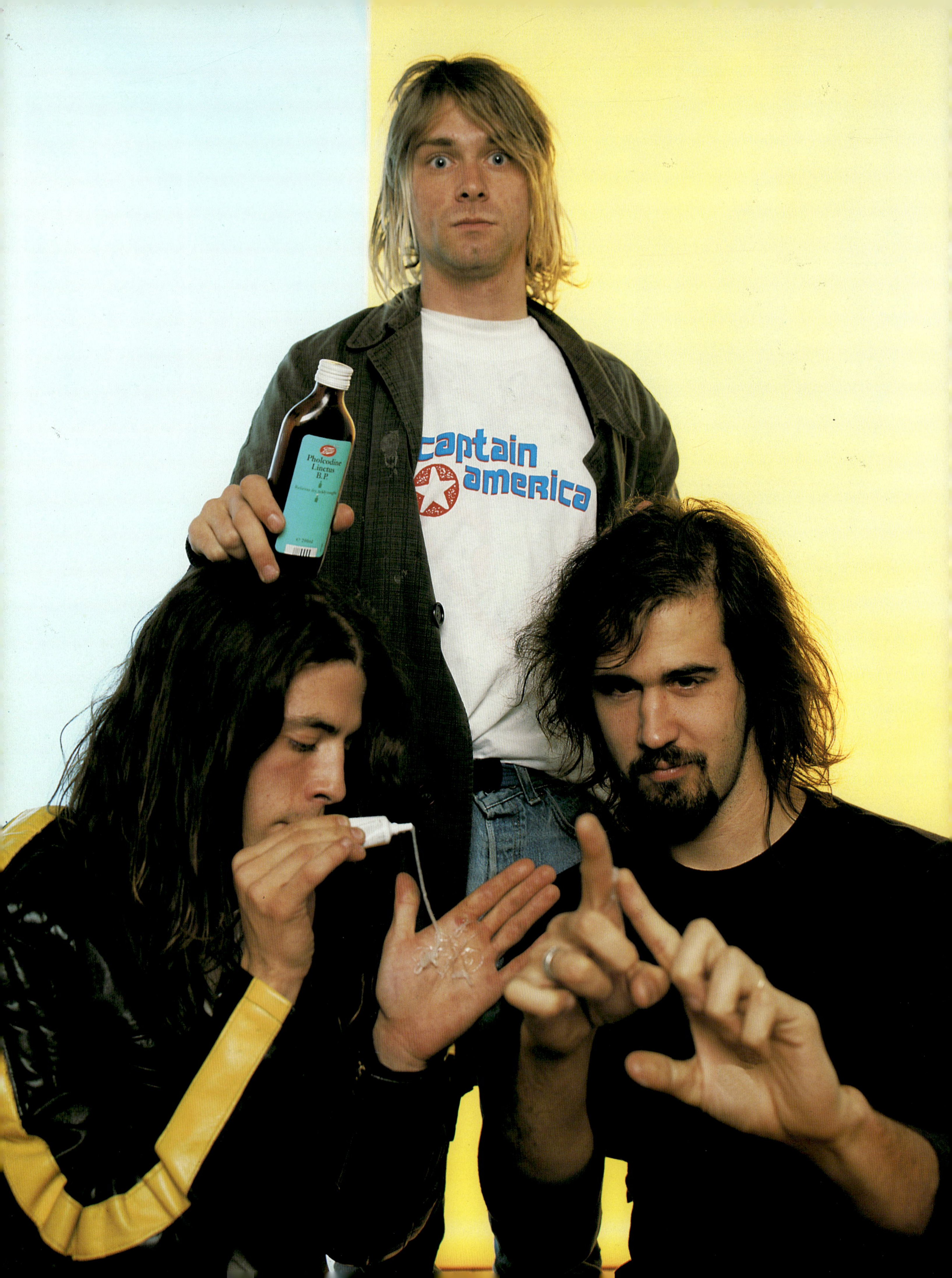
Pholcodine
Linctus
B.P.
captain
america

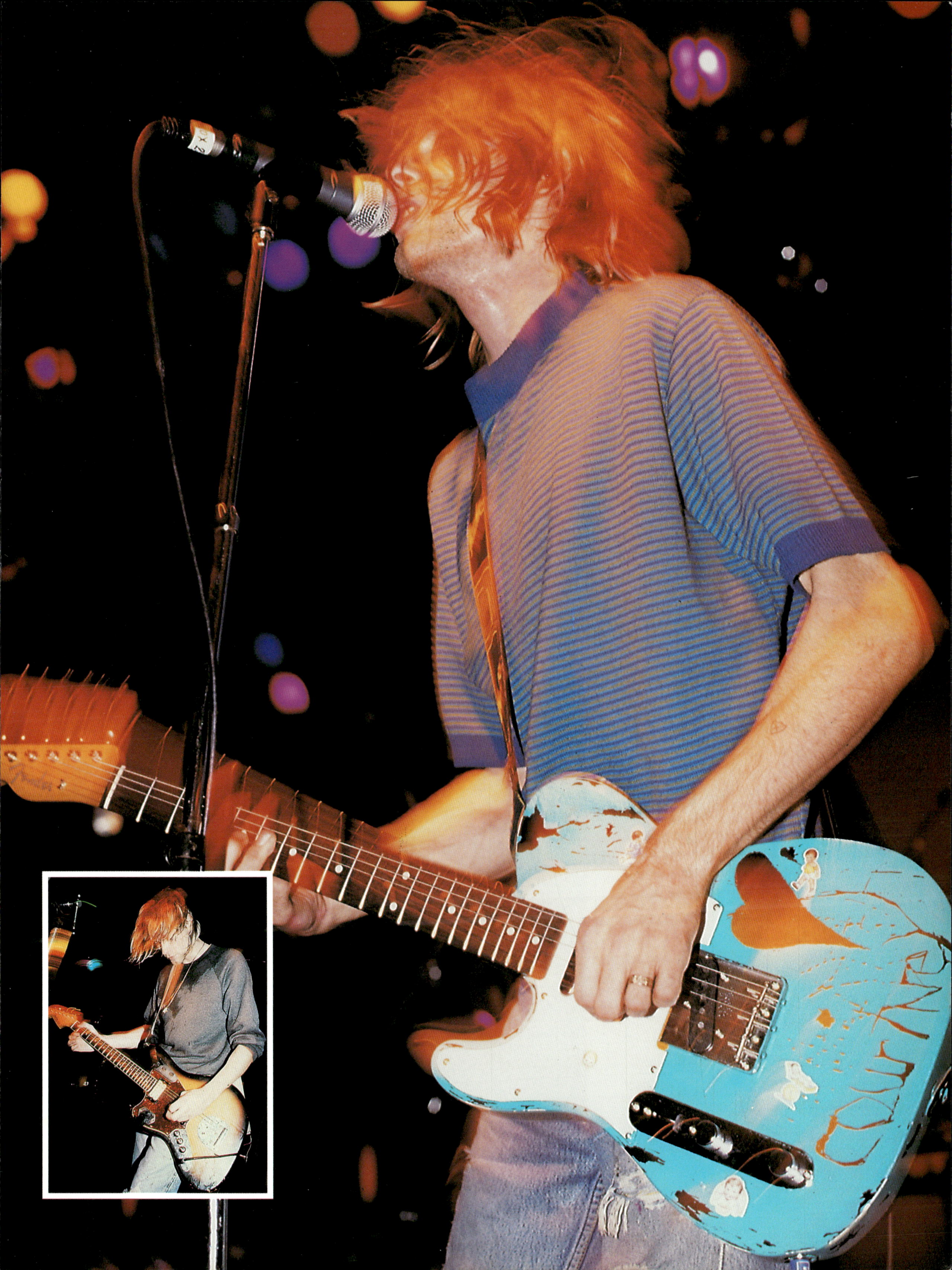

The most consistent factor in the band's progress at this time was dissension, however. Everman survived no more than a few months, before joining near-neighbours Soundgarden. Drummer Chad Channing was the next to fall, causing a proposed U.K. tour in March 1990 to be aborted. Dave Crover of The Melvins filled the vacancy for a while, as Nirvana suffered an enervating seven-week trek round the West Coast states in the back of a van; and that autumn the band returned to Europe, sharing a bill with female hard-rockers (still enough of a rarity for their sex to feature in all the advertising) L7. Mudhoney's Dan Peters was another temporary occupant of the drumstool, lasting only a matter of days. Eventually, Nirvana recruited Dave Grohl, drummer with highly regarded hardcore band Scream — who hailed from Washington (DC, that is, rather than Washington state).

As far as the outside world was concerned, 1990 was a year of stasis rather than progress for Nirvana. Beneath the surface, however, changes and decisions were being made which would determine the band's fate. The admission to the ranks of a stable percussionist was one factor; another was the conscious move towards a more accessible sound, albeit without sacrificing any of the raw energy or uncompromising world view. "We figured that we may as well get on the radio and make a little bit of money at it," Cobain explained in retrospect.

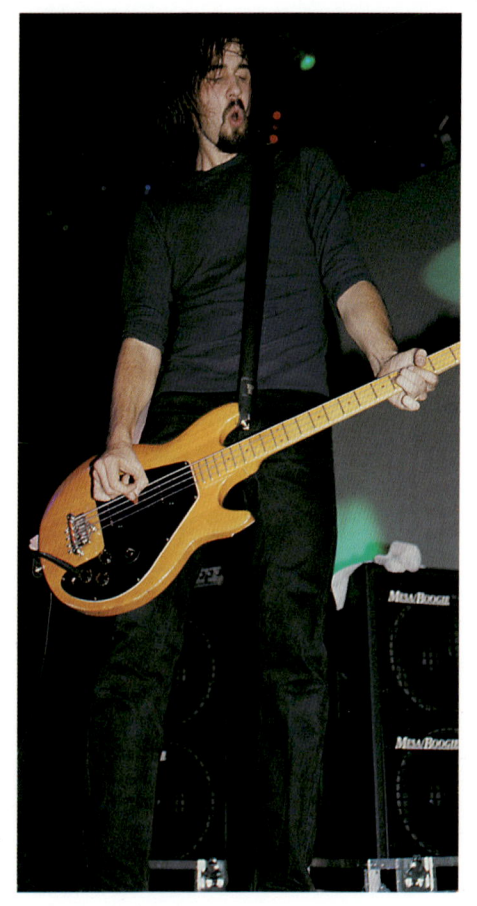

Even more vital was the business manoeuvring in which the band became embroiled that summer. Poneman and Pavitt were already searching for major label distribution for Sub Pop; but lengthy discussions with Columbia Records eventually broke down. Meanwhile, Nirvana themselves were being bombarded with offers from multi-national concerns — a total of eight majors eventually expressing a confirmed interest in signing the band. As Cobain admitted, "We got tired of waiting for the Sub Pop deal to be sorted out, so we started looking." They signed a management deal with the people who'd helped Sonic Youth land a contract with David Geffen's

DGC label; and all the way they continued to work on a second album for Sub Pop, who hadn't officially been told of Nirvana's intention to leave.

> "AMERICA MAY BE THE LAND OF THE FREE, BUT THERE ARE DEFINITELY MORE IGNORANT PEOPLE THERE. MOST OF THE POPULATION ARE SEMI-RETARDED."
> **KURT**

In the late summer of 1990, Sub Pop issued a new Nirvana single, the stunning 'Sliver'. Melodic yet devastatingly heavy, it pointed out their new direction so clearly that no-one could be confused. Sub Pop prepared to issue a follow-up in October, with the album to follow immediately afterwards; but then they received word that Nirvana had elected to follow Sonic Youth onto DGC. Sub Pop were paid off, and the deal was settled without apparent animosity on either side.

After another set of exhausting live shows, Nirvana finally found time in the spring and summer of 1991 to concentrate

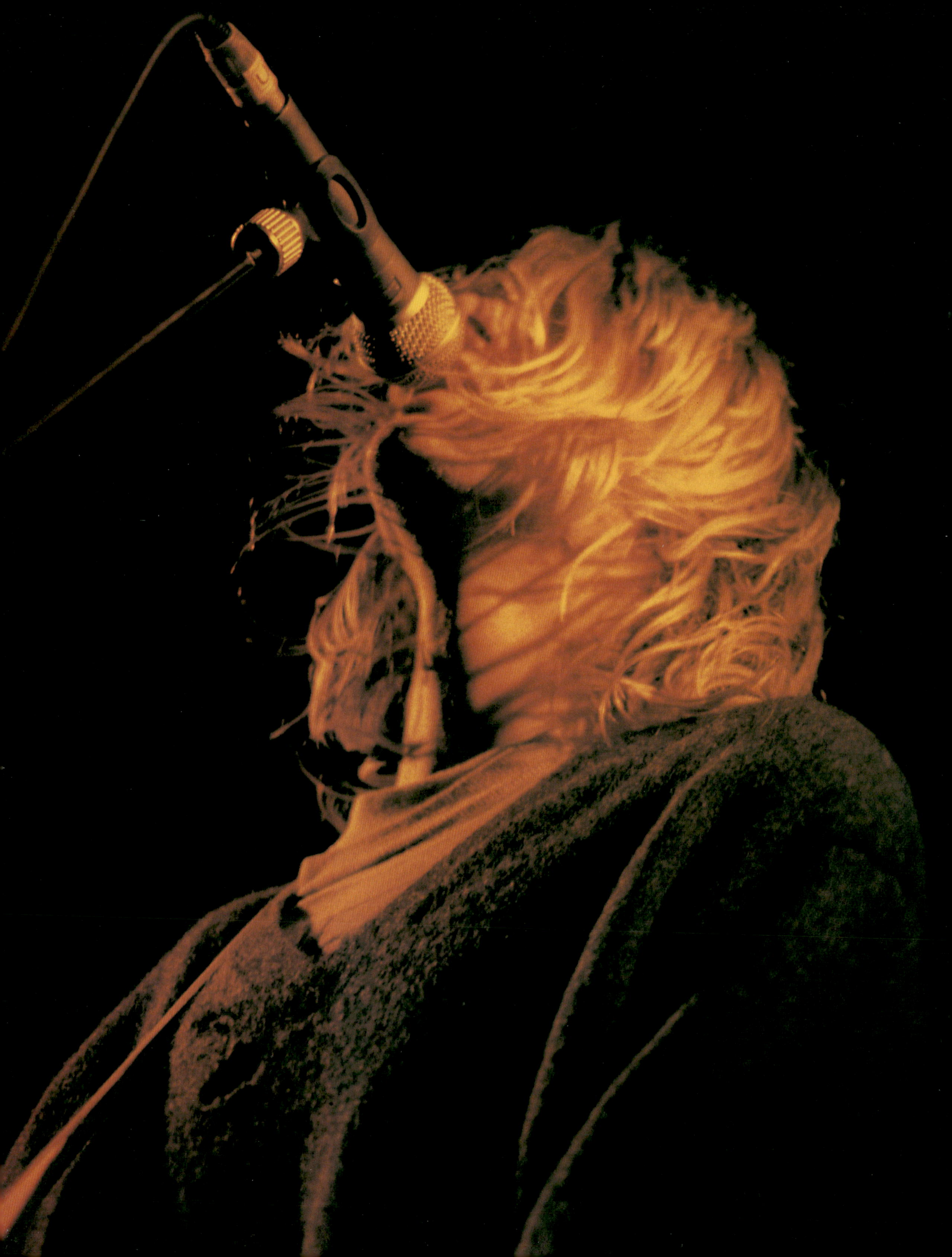

on recording. At DGC's suggestion, they were re-recording the material they'd planned to issue on Sub Pop, with underground veteran Butch Vig at the controls. He gave Nirvana a depth of sound missing from their rather one-dimensional early recordings, supporting the new melodic strength of Cobain's writing. And the final mix by Andy Wallace, best known for his work with thrash rockers Slayer, was the final gloss on a remarkable set of recordings.

Illicit copies of the rejected Sub Pop tapes had already begun to circulate in the industry by this time, so word was already spreading that the band's new material was leagues beyond their first album. The impression was confirmed in August 1991, when Nirvana appeared midway through the first day's bill at the Reading Festival, ending a devastating performance with Cobain leaping into the crowd, Novoselic throwing his bass at Grohl, and Cobain then returning to leap into the midst of Grohl's drumkit.

"MAINTAINING THE PUNK ROCK ETHOS IS MORE IMPORTANT TO ME THAN ANYTHING."
— KURT

On September 24th 1991, 'Nevermind' reached the shops in America — or at least 50,000 copies of the album did, a comparatively modest first run by major label standards in the States. Reviewers raved universally, on both sides of the Atlantic; but what tipped the balance was MTV's decision to run the lead video from the album in full on their massively influential 120 Minutes showcase for new underground talent. The song in question was 'Smells Like Teen Spirit', and the video caused such a reaction that it was quickly switched to heavy rotation on the mainstream MTV shows, alongside new

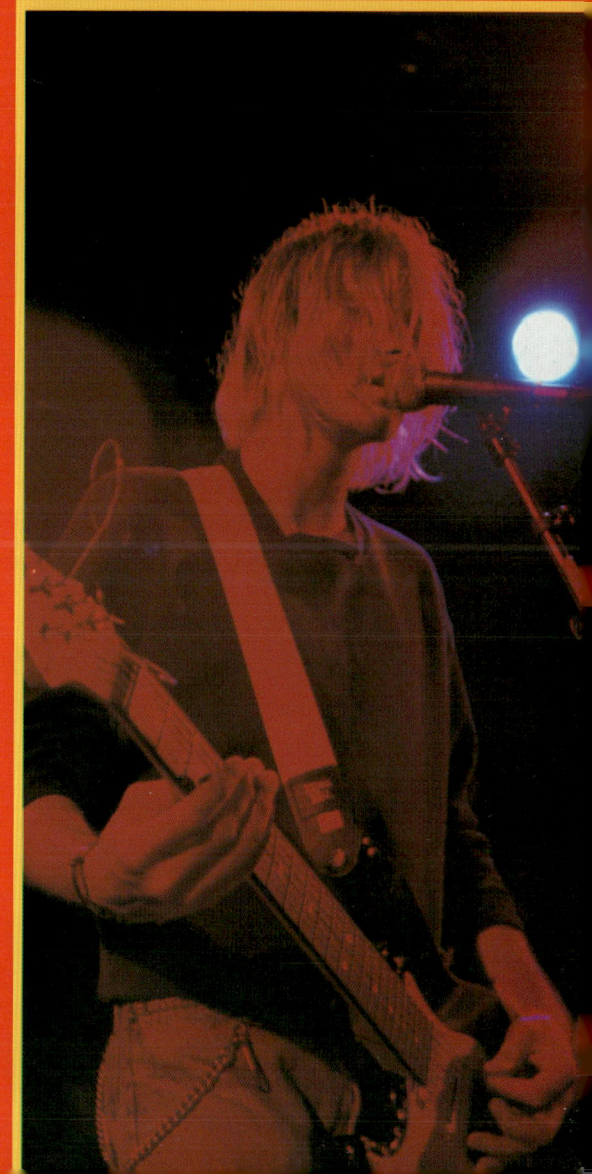

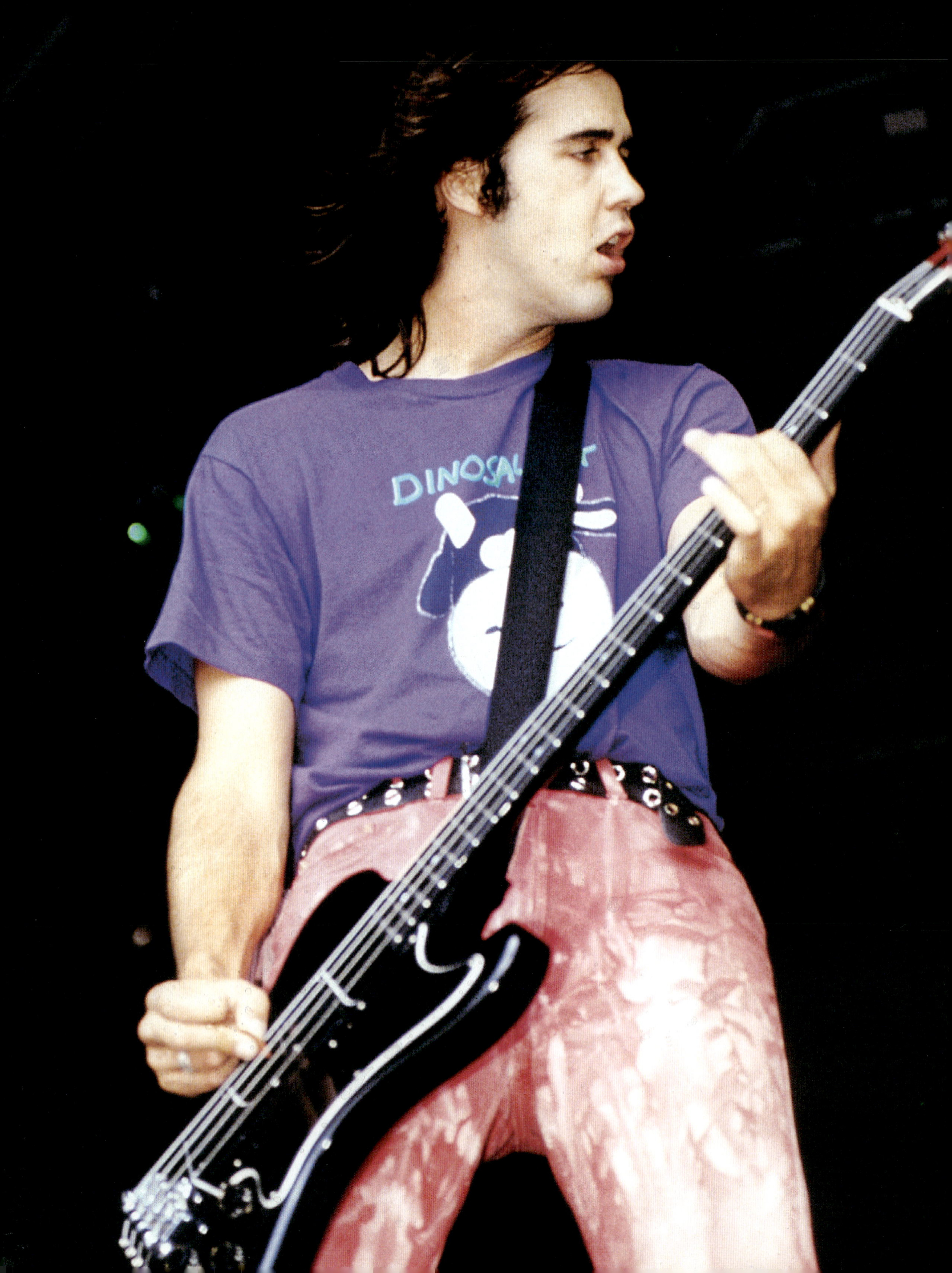

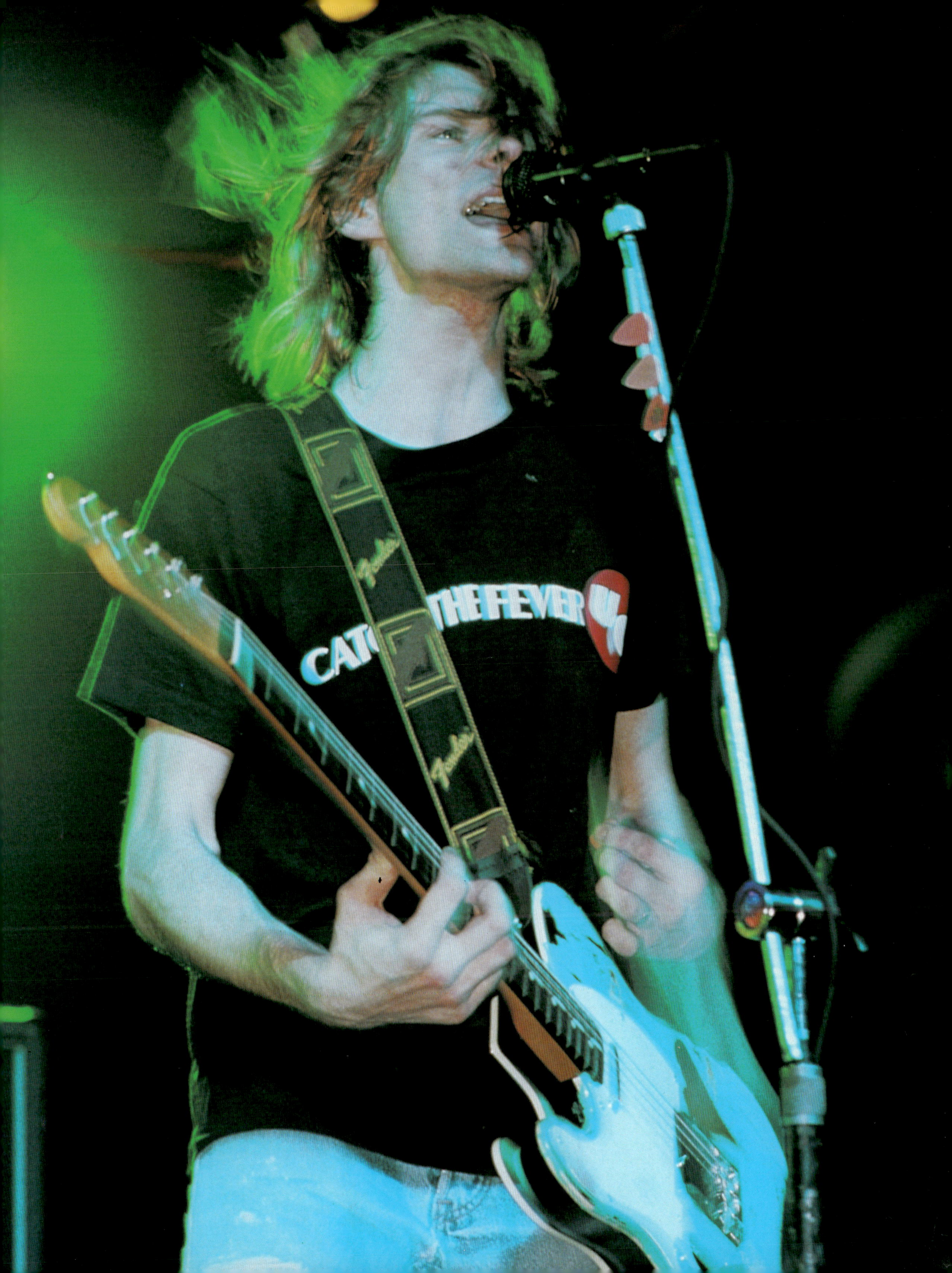

CATC
THE FEVER
Fender
Fender

kiss between Kurt and Chris, a moment broadcast live that night but cut from later airings of the show.

On February 24, 1992, Kurt Cobain married his girlfriend Courtney Love in Waikiki, Hawaii, in a ceremony conducted by a nondenominational female minister; their witness was a roadie. Kurt wore his pyjamas. Courtney, born Love Michelle Harrison, was the daughter of a Grateful Dead roadie and a therapist, and by all reports had an unusual upbringing — as she says, "I was raised by white trash that considered themselves hippies." Kurt's new wife attended Woodstock at the ripe old age of three and allegedly dropped acid at her parent's suggestion before she was old enough to go to school. Love had

> "I DON'T KNOW HOW MUCH LONGER I CAN SCREAM AT THE TOP OF MY LUNGS EVERY NIGHT FOR AN ENTIRE YEAR ON TOUR."
> **KURT**

her own band, named Hole, whose first album 'Pretty On The Inside' was released one week before 'Nevermind' in the States, and on the same day in Britain. Before she kick-started her musical career she had earned her living as a stripper. A wild, strong-willed woman, Courtney would aid in bringing even more publicity to Nirvana in the months to come.

In April, Courtney Love revealed that she was pregnant and expecting a child in just a few months, and on August 18, 1992, Frances Bean Cobain was born in Los Angeles. The healthy baby girl was the subject of controversy before she was even born, and the bomb dropped when Vanity Fair's September issue hit the newsstands. Featuring a photograph of Love, very pregnant and wearing transparent lingerie (the cigarette in her hand air-brushed away), the glossy magazine's article contained quotes from the mother-to-be that were to cast a thundercloud over the Cobains' new-found parenthood. Journalist Lynn Hirschberg painted a picture of a "train-wreck personality," but

releases by the likes of Genesis and Guns N' Roses.

'Nevermind' began to sell upwards of 70,000 copies a day, rapidly went double platinum, and then in January 1992 knocked Michael Jackson's over-hyped 'Dangerous' off the top of the US album charts. Success in Britain was equally impressive, with 'Smells Like Teen Spirit' entering the Top 10, followed quickly by 'Come As You Are'. Nirvana was reaching listeners who had given up on hard rock and metal years before.

The mounting hysteria accompanied the band on the road, where they jetted deliriously around the world on a six-month schedule that came close to crushing them in its tracks. They were in Britain in November, again in December, and back in February, with a return to the Reading Festival booked for August. The tour moved on through Europe, Australia, New Zealand, Japan and Hawaii.

> "PUNK ROCK IS, TO ME, DEAD AND GONE."
> **KURT**

In between, they galloped around the States, starting the year off with a bang with a memorable New Year's Eve gig in California, where they blew headliners the Red Hot Chili Peppers offstage. The band then played in front of all of America on Saturday Night Live, finishing off their performance (after the obligatory smashing-up of their equipment) with a flourish in the form of a "French"

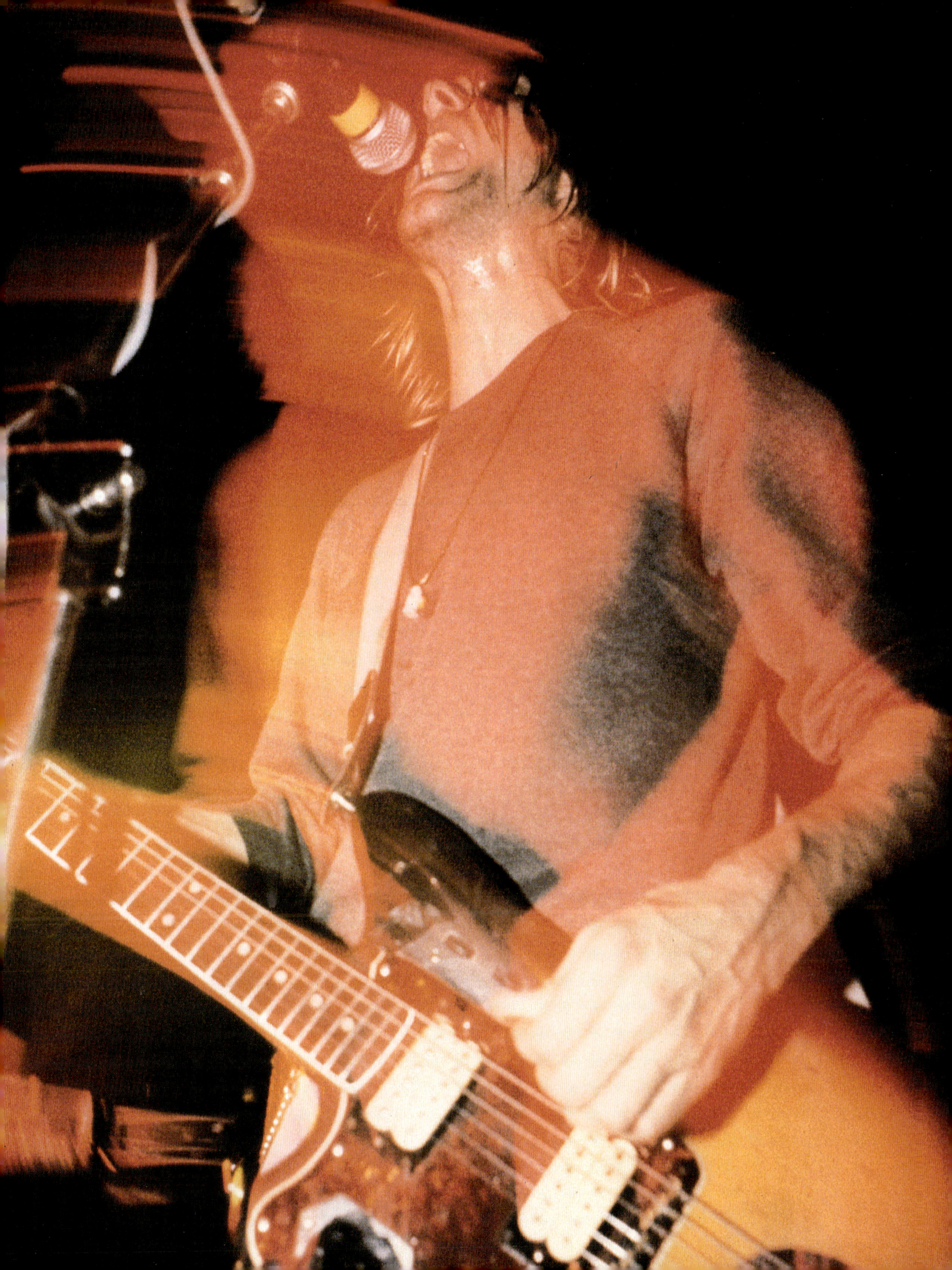

the truly damning lightning bolt came from Courtney herself. She was quoted, when asked about what she and Kurt had been up to at the start of the year, as saying "We went on a binge. We did a lot of drugs . . . we got high and did Saturday Night Live. After that, I did heroin for a couple of months." This was proof, as far as Hirschberg was concerned, that Love had admitted to having used heroin while pregnant.

Kurt and Courtney knew as soon as they read the article — before its publication — that it would cause irreparable damage. "The power of it was so intense," Love said. "I read a fax of it and my bones shook. I knew that my world was over." Unable to deal with the horror she felt due to the article, Courtney checked herself into the hospital for the last two weeks of her pregnancy. Kurt himself was

> "I DON'T THINK COURTNEY AND I ARE THAT FUCKED UP. WE HAVE JUST LACKED LOVE ALL OUR LIVES."
> **KURT**

hospitalized at the time of his daughter's birth; he was detoxing. The couple issued a statement the day before the condemning article was published, and in response to the allegations that Courtney used drugs when she knew she was pregnant, the Cobains asserted, "We unequivocally deny this."

But it was too late. The Globe's headline was "Rock Star's Baby Is Born A Junkie." The Los Angeles County Department of Children's Services threatened to take Frances Bean out of her parent's custody, and what should have been a time for celebration turned into a nightmare.

Just ten days after Kurt became a father, Nirvana played the U.K. Reading Festival. In September the band performed at the MTV Video Music Awards, and received two awards: Best Alternative Video for 'Smells Like Teen Spirit' and Best New Artists. Typically,

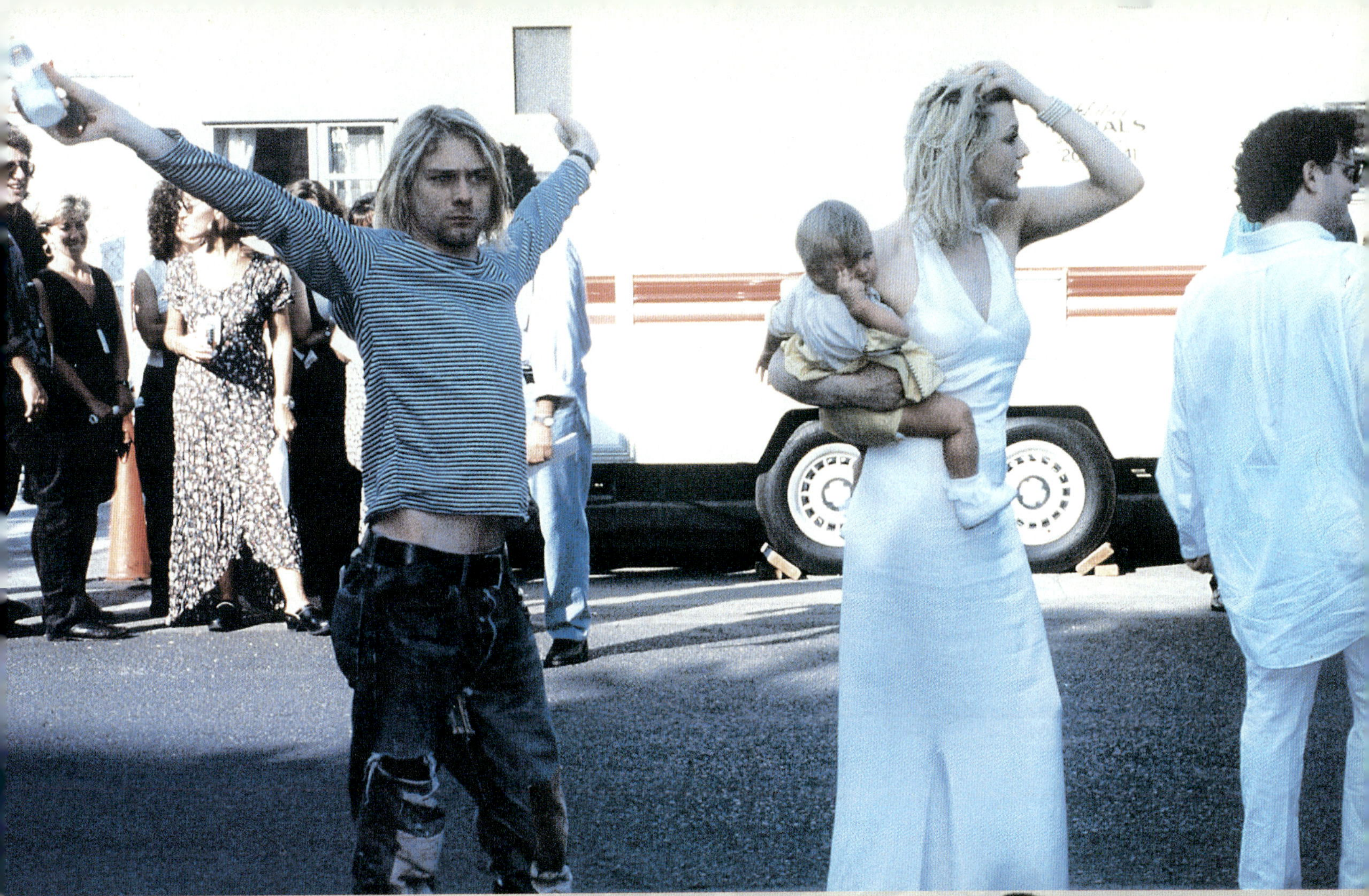

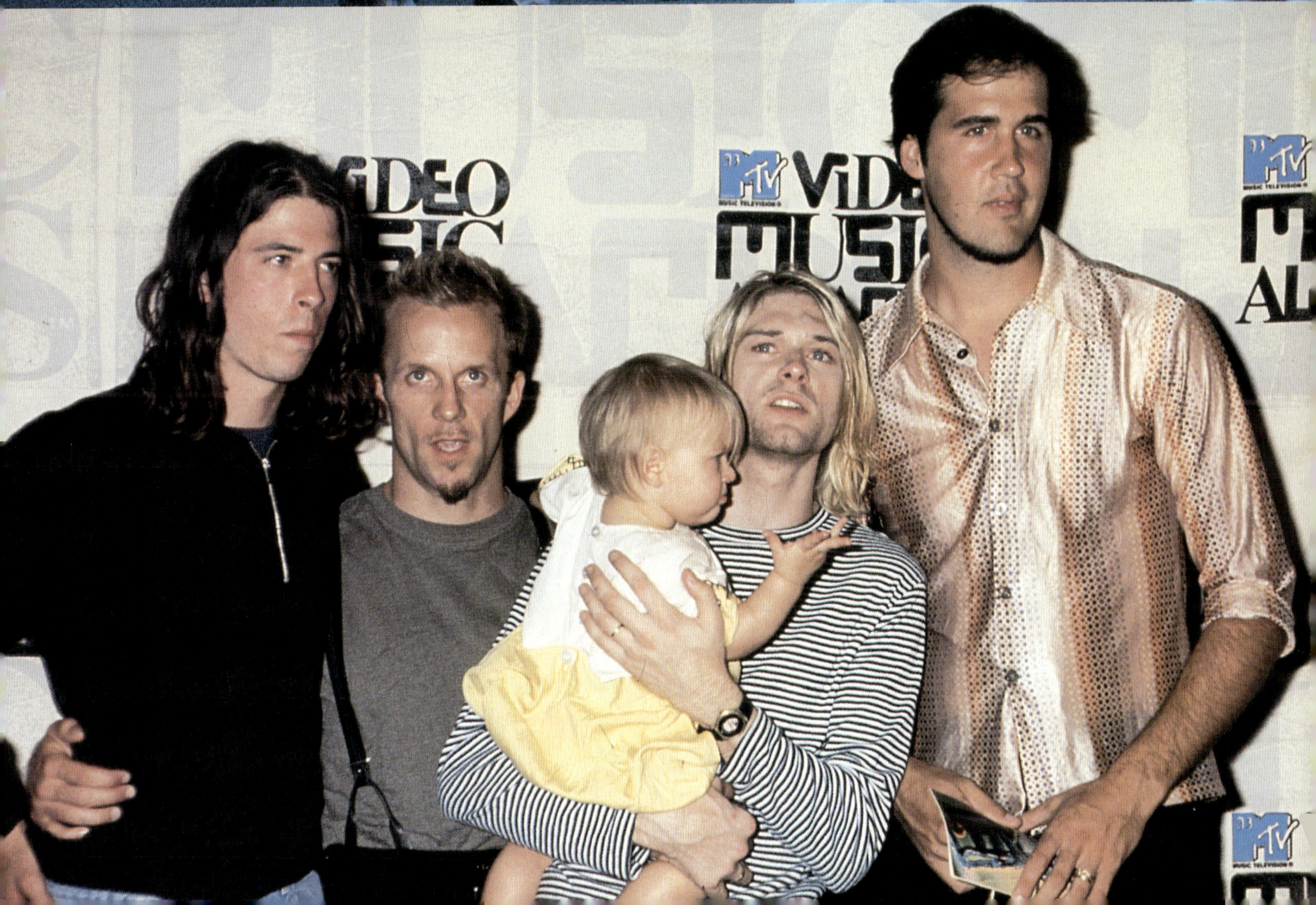
MTV
MUSIC TELEVISION
VIDEO
MUSIC

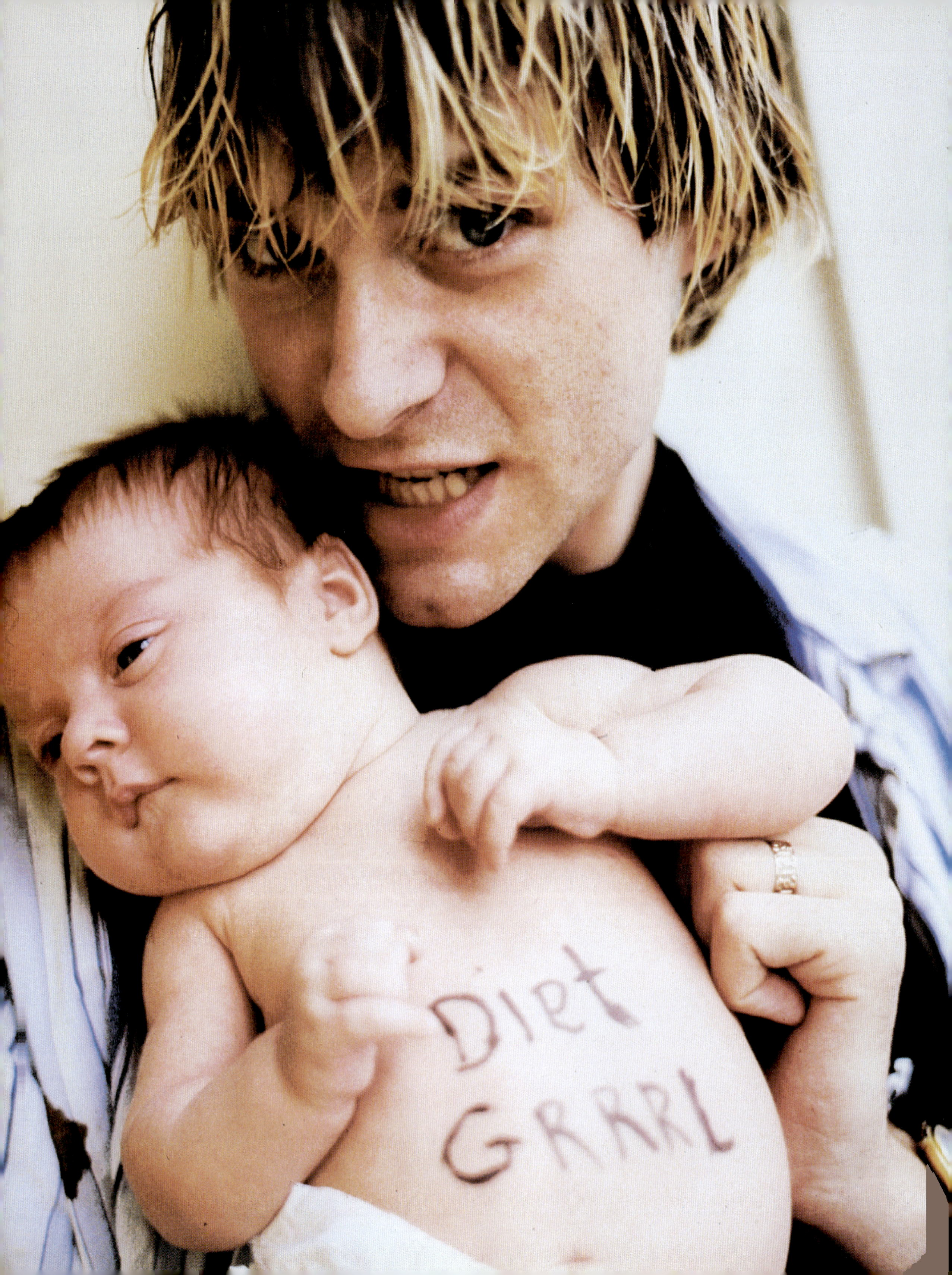
Diet
GRRRL

the evening did not go without a bit of drama: Kurt and Courtney were reportedly "threatened" by Axl Rose of Guns N' Roses backstage, and Nirvana was banned from playing the song 'Rape Me' as per a ruling by MTV bigwigs.

> "NOW I HAVE THIS HUGE RESPONSIBILITY TO MY FAMILY, AND IT'S PROBABLY MORE PRESSURE THAN I'VE EVER HAD DEALING WITH THIS BAND."
> **KURT**

The band's incredible rise to world-wide stardom was the source of begrudgery amongst some parties. Long-time admirers claimed the band had sold out by signing with a major label. Britain's New Musical Express described Nirvana as "The Guns N' Roses it's OK to like," and heavy metal magazine Kerrang!'s line was "Nevermind The Bollocks, Here's the Success Pistols." Despite some resentment, however, it was difficult to brush aside the fact that here was a band that had redefined the concept of "mainstream" music. While bands like REM and U2 had crafted a place for "alternative" music for the masses, they had done so through years of critically acclaimed — if not immediately commercially successful — records and had developed strong cult status through years of touring. In Nirvana, here was a band who had seemingly foregone all of the preliminaries and had crashed into the world of pop music without concession, and indeed without intent, changing the face of mainstream music forever.

"All we did was put out a record last September," muttered Chris Novoselic in baffled response to world-wide Nirvanamania. But what a record it was: a staggering barrage of riffs and hooks, linked with lyrics that explored the ennui of American youth in the Bush era, the terrifying consequences of macho behaviour and the sheer terror of being alive.

To be suddenly and unexpectedly the most popular band in the world would send any group of musicians into a tailspin, but for Kurt, Chris and Dave the adjustment was even more difficult due to the fact that they weren't quite sure that they *wanted* to be the most popular band in the world. They began moaning about their frenetic tour schedule, and the pressure was evident in the ever-increasing fury with which they destroyed instruments at the end of every gig; the $750 weekly equipment damage allowance set for the band at the beginning of the tour became laughable.

Kurt in particular grew increasingly disenchanted with the press, the public and Nirvana itself. Unable to grasp the concept that once you have sold millions of albums you forfeit the right to hand-pick the people who name themselves amongst your fans, Kurt launched a campaign against record-buyers and concert-goers

> "I'M DISGUSTED WITH HAVING TO DEAL WITH THE COMMERCIAL SIDE OF OUR BAND AT THE MOMENT, AND AS A REACTION I'M BECOMING MORE UPTIGHT AND COMPLAIN MORE."
> **KURT**

who did not conform to his own beliefs. Dismayed that people who were, in his eyes, racists, intolerant of gays or lacking in true appreciation of his music, Kurt pleaded that they "leave us the fuck alone — don't come to our shows and don't buy our records."

As if the Vanity Fair episode weren't enough, yet another case of the written word causing the Cobains heartache came along in the form of a Nirvana biography by Victoria Clarke and Britt Collins. Although Kurt and Courtney seemed willing to cooperate with the project early in 1992, once it was revealed that the authors had spoken with Lynn Hirschberg, all relations between the Cobains and the writers disintegrated. The thought of having yet more damaging text available for all to read prompted a violent reaction from the Cobains. A series of threatening messages were left by

> "I HAVE TO HEAR RUMORS ABOUT ME ALL THE TIME, I'M TOTALLY FUCKING SICK OF IT."
> **KURT**

both Courtney and Kurt on Clarke's answering machine; the messages were later published in the U.K. music magazine Select early in 1993. Love was quoted as saying, "We will use every dollar we have and every bit of our power to basically fuck you up." Kurt's message, as quoted, was perhaps less bullying if more desperate: "...if anything comes out in this book which hurts my wife, I'll fucking hurt you." It was even alleged that Courtney met up with Clarke in a bar in Hollywood and assaulted her.

Kurt issued an "open letter" near the close of 1992 — a year in which more had happened to Cobain, Love and Nirvana than could ever have been predicted. The aim of this statement was to clear the air and the Cobains' reputations, but it seemed that a snowball effect had taken hold and wasn't letting go. "We are decent, ethical people," Kurt insisted in his letter. Whether anyone chose to believe him or not, he, his family and his band had become public property. The end of the year saw media coverage of Nirvana and its ever-spreading realm of influence reach an alltime high. From Vogue magazine's feature of the grunge look as seen on the runways to Entertainment Weekly's cover story in which Courtney continued her attack in print against Nirvana's unofficial biographers, Nirvana was everywhere.

In the midst of all of this turmoil, Nirvana was still a band, and in October they began demo recording sessions for their new album with producer Jack Endino. At the end of the year, Incesticide, an album compilation of B-sides, rare Sub Pop tracks and demos was released. The album's artwork included forwarding notes penned by Kurt himself in his inimitable caustic style. Citing the few events in his recent life that had transcended any joy he may have felt due to commercial success (searching for back-issues of the New Musical Express in London, aiding the career of Shonen Knife and meeting Iggy Pop), Kurt's words were engagingly candid. He closes with a mention of the now-infamous Saturday Night Live gig, recalling kissing Kris and Dave "just to spite homophobes."

Working with producer Steve Albini, Nirvana recorded basic tracks for their

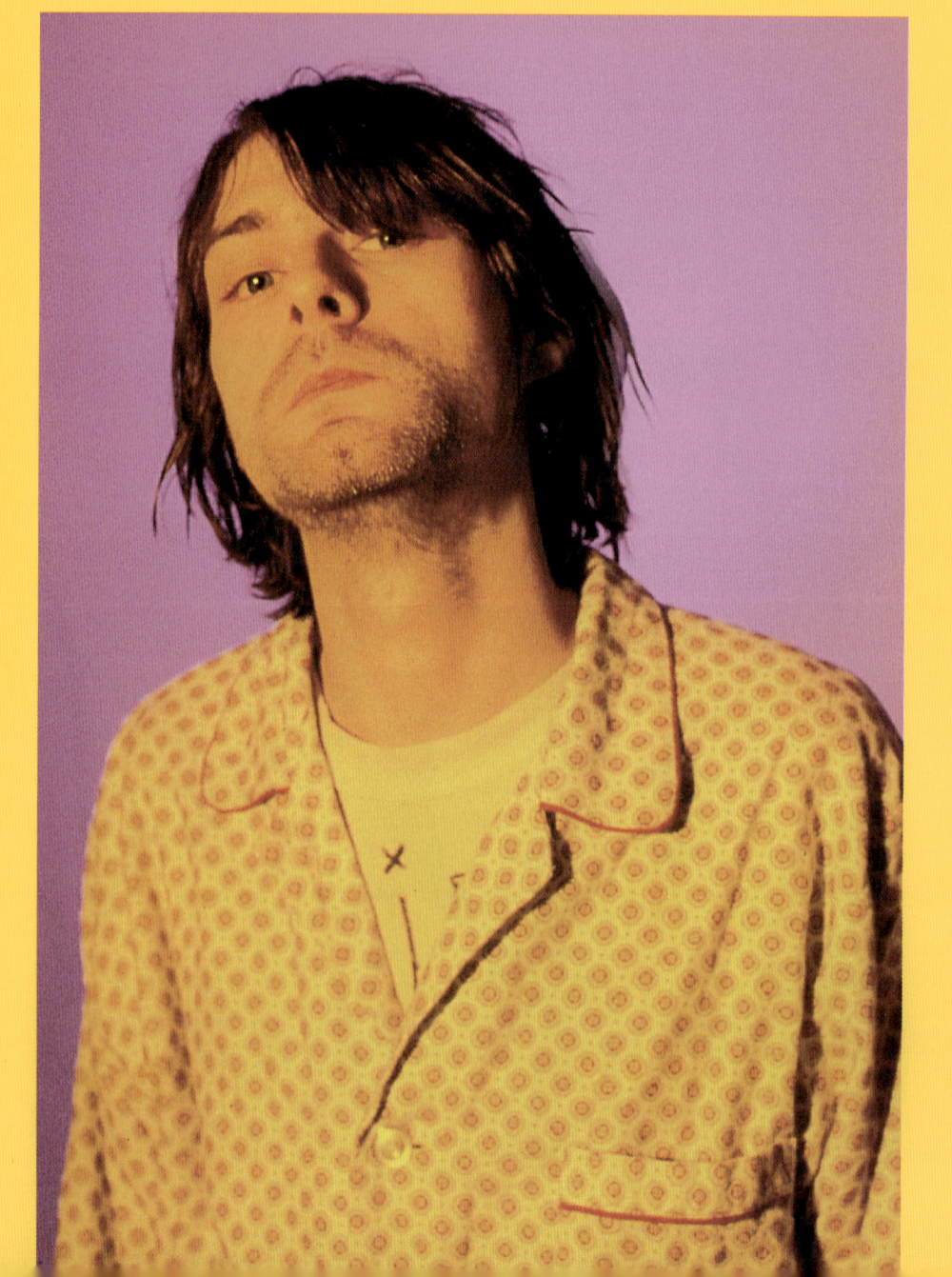

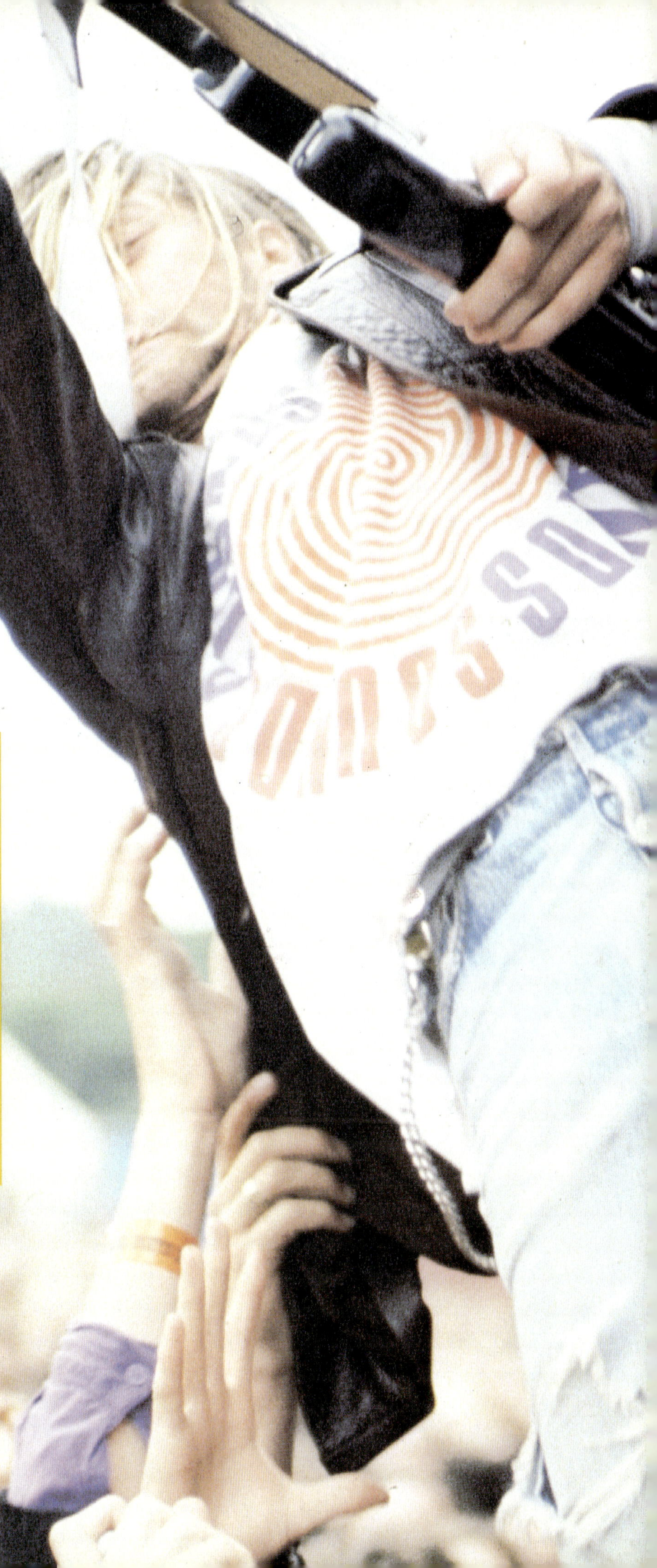

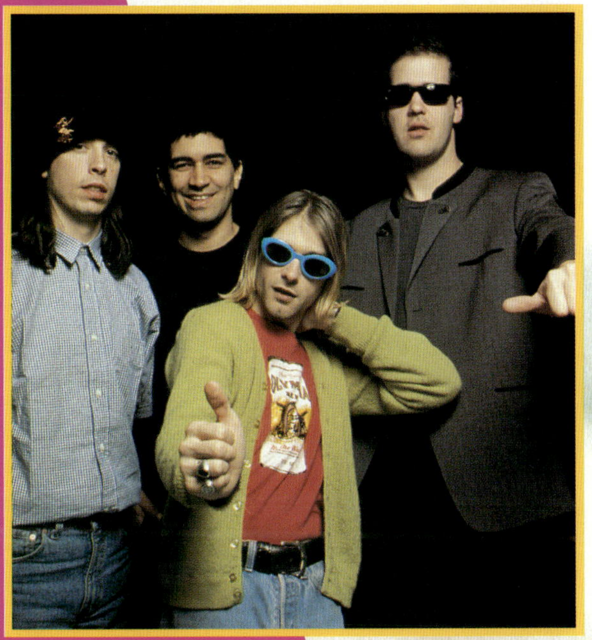

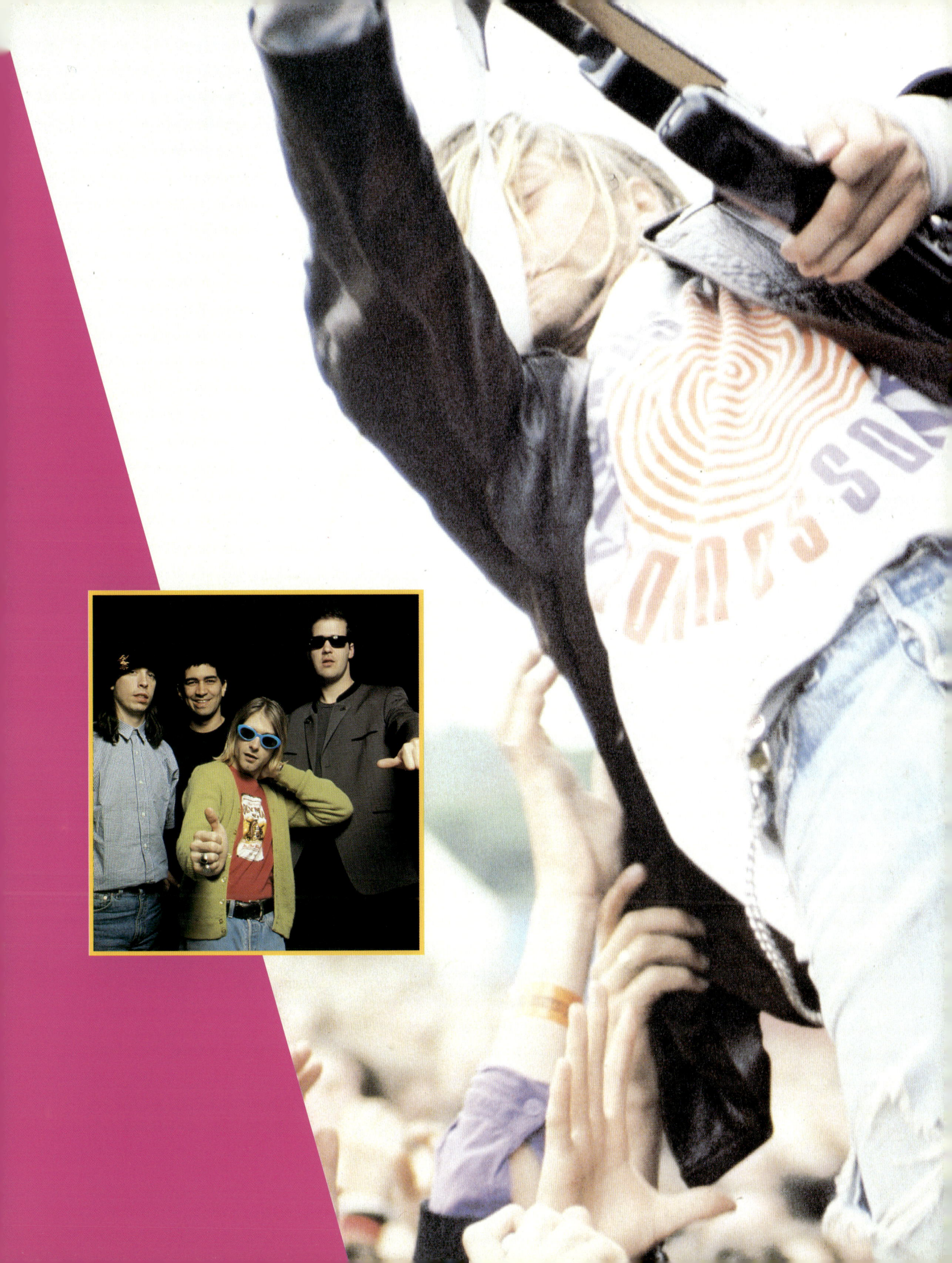

upcoming album in just three days in mid-February 1993 at Pachyderm Studios in Minnesota. The working title of the album was, chillingly enough in retrospect, 'I Hate Myself And I Want To Die'.

Released in the Fall of 1993 under the title 'In Utero', Nirvana's fourth album was a feast of introspective and often jaded lyrics; Kurt's songwriting had become at once more sophisticated and more self-involved. As powerful and as successful as its predecessor, 'Nevermind', the album was critically acclaimed and topped the charts with uncanny speed. Filled with phrases documenting a disturbed state of mind: "Look on the bright side is suicide," "I am my own parasite" and "I wish I could eat your cancer when you turn black," Cobain's words were to take on an even darker meaning in the year to come. In testimony to his ever-increasing dissatisfaction with commercial success was the song 'Radio Friendly Unit Shifter' which cleverly misquoted Sinéad O'Conner's hit album with the line "I do not want what I have got." O'Conner would later record a cover version of the last track from In Utero, 'All Apologies'.

Several months of heavy touring commenced in support of the new album, and despite Kurt's continued discomfort at

> "WHEN I WRITE A SONG, THE LYRICS ARE THE LEAST IMPORTANT THING."
> **KURT**

playing sold-out shows to legions of fans each night, Nirvana played consistently well. It seemed that the lead singer of the most influential band of the decade had perhaps come to terms with his malcon-

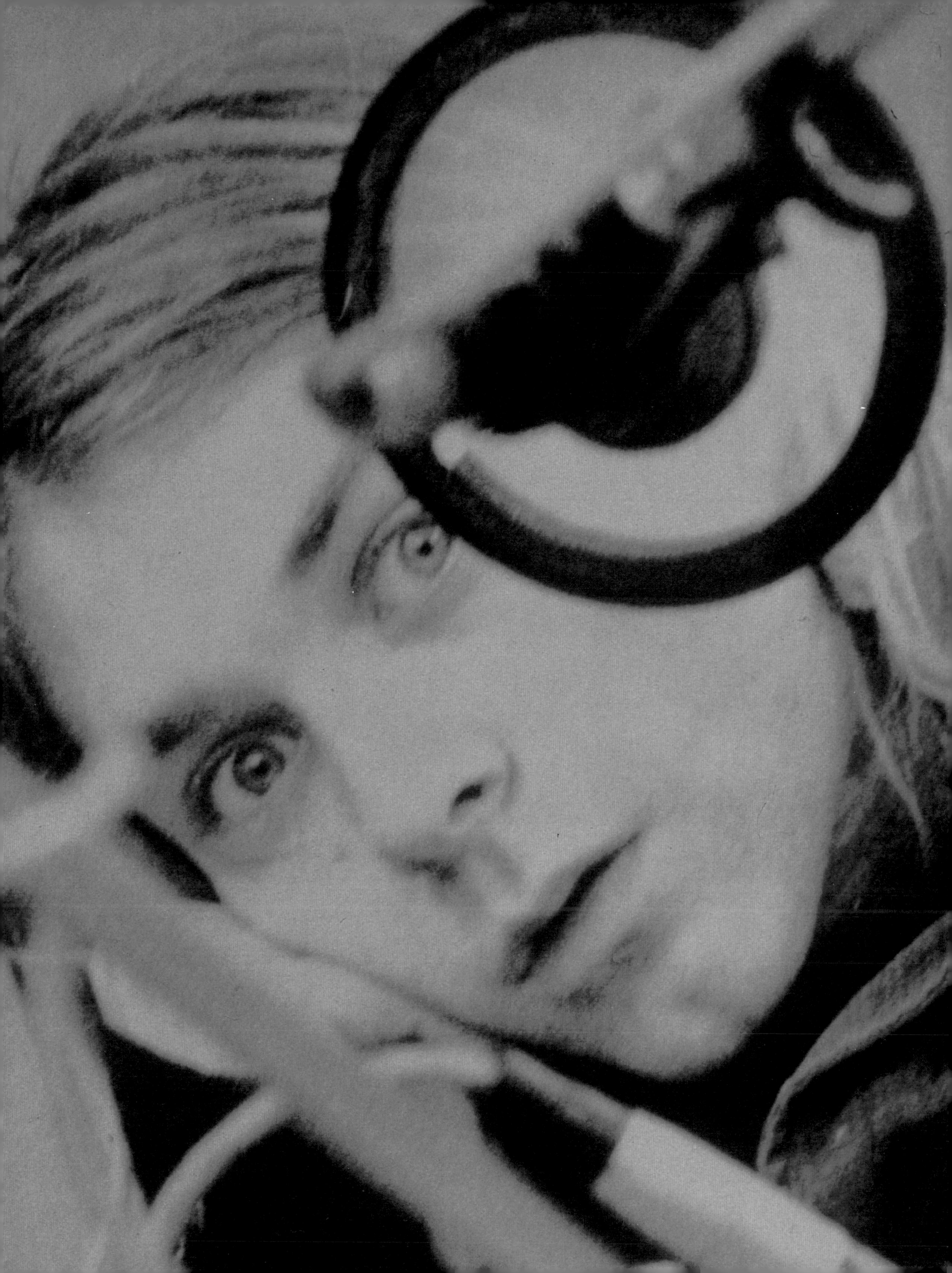

> "I'M DEFINITELY GAY IN SPIRIT AND I PROBABLY COULD BE BISEXUAL. IF I WOULDN'T HAVE FOUND COURTNEY, I PROBABLY WOULD HAVE CARRIED ON WITH A BISEXUAL LIFESTYLE."
> **KURT**

tent; he was even quoted, in early 1994, as saying, "I've never been happier in my life. I'm a much happier guy than a lot of people think I am."

On March 4, 1994, it became clear to the world that this was not in fact the case. News spread quickly that Kurt Cobain was in a drug-induced coma in a hospital in Rome. Courtney Love had called for help from their hotel room in the night as she was unable to waken her husband. Rumours of attempted suicide abounded while Cobain remained unconscious. Nirvana's management, Gold Mountain, issued a statement to the effect that it was an unfortunate accident due to Kurt's inadvertently mixing "prescription pain killers" with alcohol. After a day or so he regained consciousness and was responding to the outside world, and he checked out of the hospital on March 8 to disappear from the public eye with his wife and child.

Ten days later Love again had to summon outside help when Cobain retreated to a locked room with the company of three guns. When the police arrived, Kurt insisted that he was not suicidal; the police confiscated the guns along with two dozen boxes of ammunition.

Shortly thereafter Kurt was willingly admitted into a drug rehabilitation centre in Hollywood. He began intervention therapy, a method in which an addict is forced to face up to his problem through encounters with those close to him. After just two days of such confrontations with family and the members of the band, Kurt was unable to deal with the therapy and, as if he were an inmate in jail,

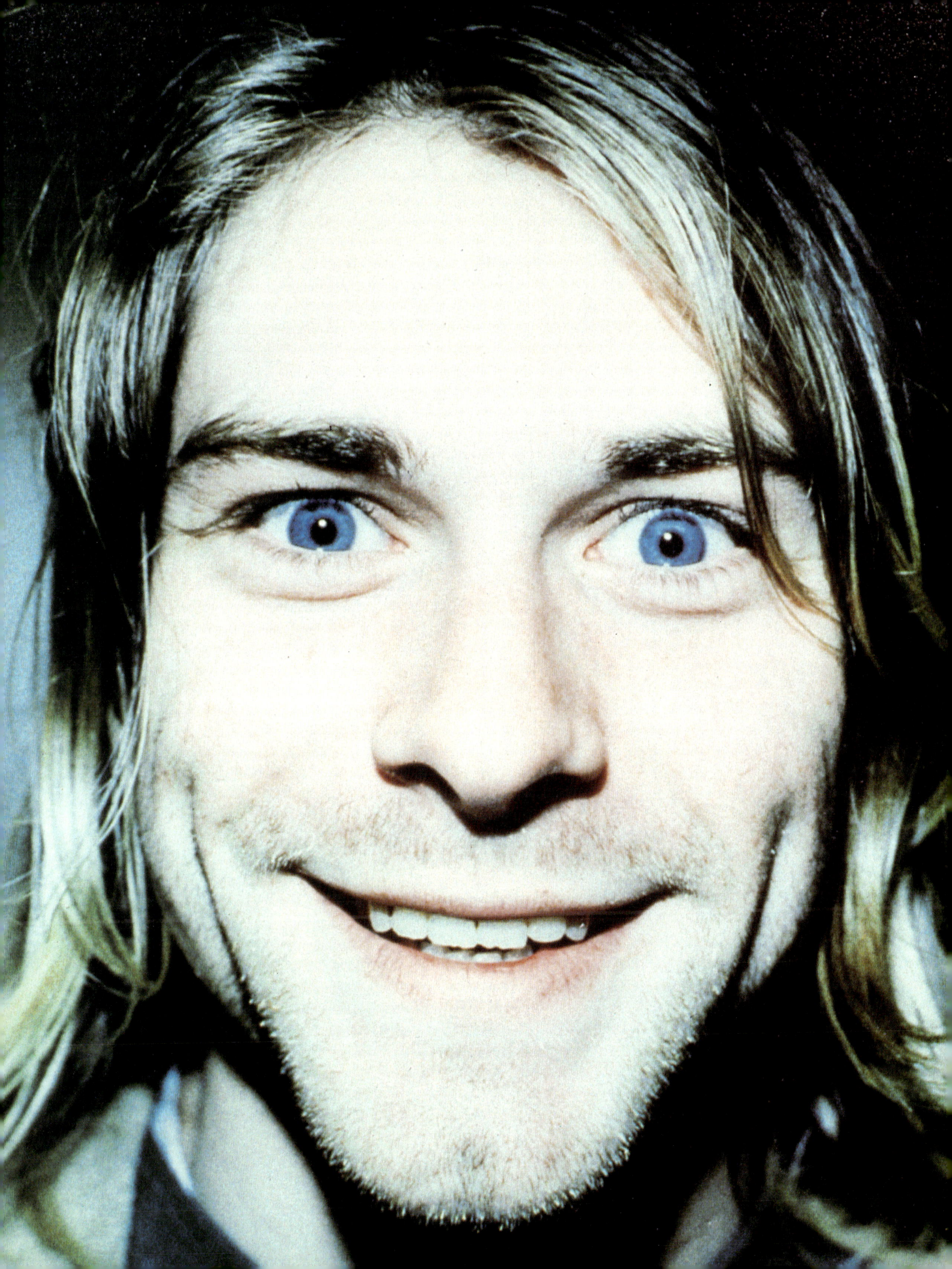

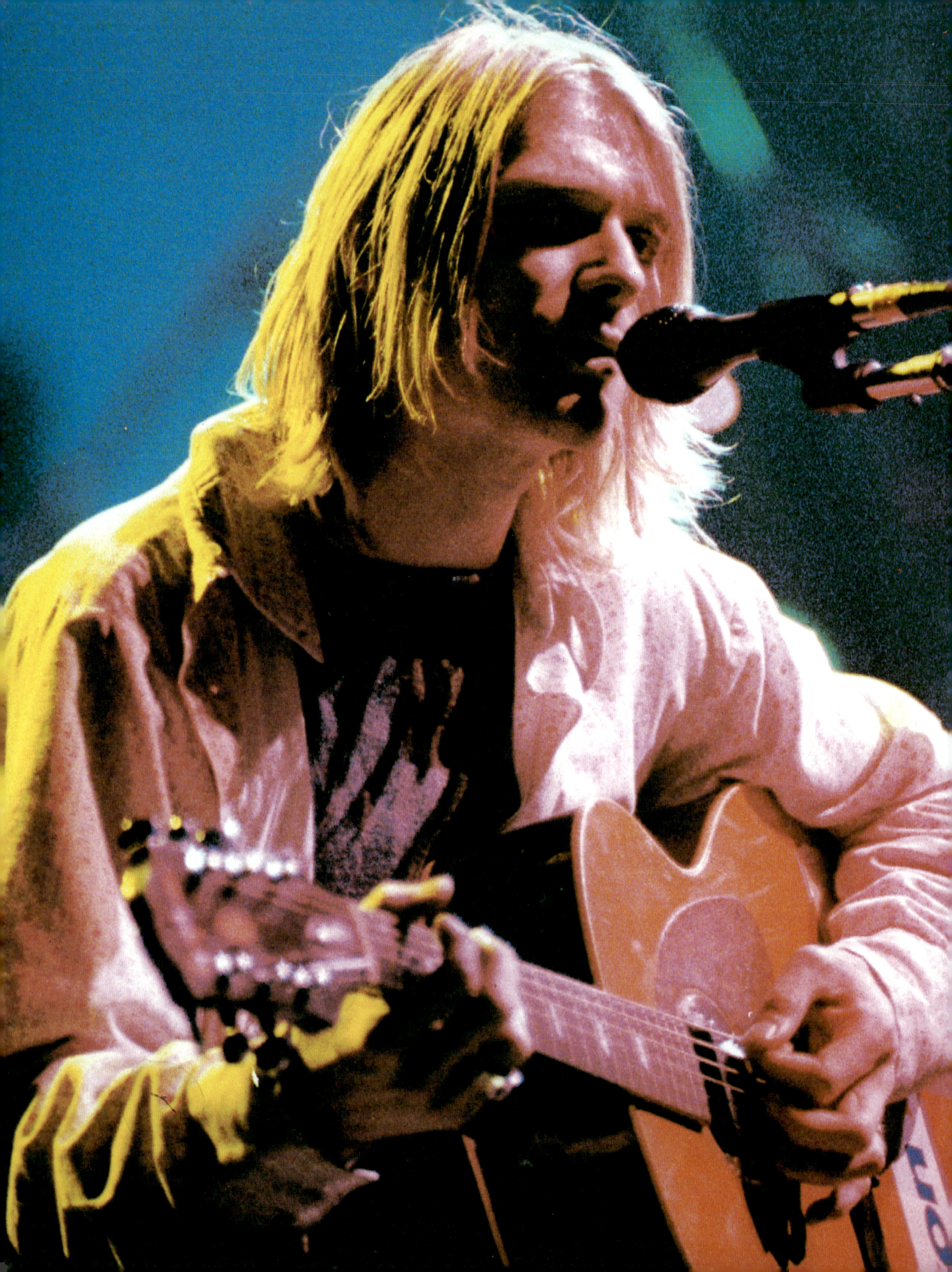

> Speaking from the tongue of an experienced simpleton who obviously would rather be an emasculated, infantile complainee. This note should be pretty easy to understand. All the warnings from the punk rock 101 courses over the years, since my first introduction to the, shall we say, ethics involved with independence and the embracement of your community has proven to be very true. I haven't felt the excitement of listening to as well as creating music along with reading and writing for too many years now. I feel guilty beyond words about these things. For example when we're back stage and the lights go out and the manic roar of the crowd begins it doesn't affect me the way in which it did for Freddy Mercury who seemed to love, relish in the love and adoration from the crowd which is something I totally admire and envy. The fact is, I can't fool you, any one of you. It simply isn't fair to you or me. The worst crime I can think of would be to rip people off by faking it and pretending as if I'm having 100% fun. Sometimes I feel as if I should have a punch in time clock before I walk out on stage. I've tried everything within my power to to appreciate it (and I do, God, believe me I do, but it's not enough). I appreciate the fact that I and we have affected and entertained a lot of people. I must be one of those narcissists who only appreciate things when they're gone. I'm too sensitive. I need to be slightly numb in order to regain the enthusiasm I once had as a child. On our last 3 tours I've had a much better appreciation for all the people I've known personally and as fans of our music, but I still can't get over the frustration, the guilt and empathy I have for everyone. There's good in all of us and I think I simply love people too much. So much that it makes me feel too fucking sad. The sad little, sensitive, unappreciative, pisces, Jesus man! Why don't you just enjoy it? I don't know! I have a goddess of a wife who sweats ambition and empathy and a daughter who reminds me too much of what I used to be. Full of love and joy, kissing every person she meets because everyone is good and will do her no harm. And that terrifies me to the point to where I can barely function. I can't stand the thought of Frances becoming the miserable self destructive, death rocker that I've become. I have it good, very good, and I'm grateful, but since the age of seven I've become hateful towards all humans in general. Only because it seems so easy for people to get along and have empathy. Empathy! Only because I love and feel for people too much I guess. Thank you all from the pit of my burning nauseous stomach for your letters and concern during the past years. I'm too much of an erratic, moody baby! I don't have the passion anymore and so remember, it's better to burn out than to fade away.
>
> Peace, love, Empathy. Kurt Cobain

"escaped" by jumping over a fence. He did not contact anyone for days.

Cobain's mother filed a missing persons report and Love reportedly employed a private investigator. "He is probably going to turn up dead and join that stupid club I told him not to join," Kurt's mother told reporters, alluding to the ever-growing number of musicians who have died young at their own hand.

Although the Seattle house Kurt and Courtney had moved into at the beginning of the year was periodically checked, the only sightings of the missing rock star were by neighbours who claimed to have seen him wandering about in a park close by, wearing a heavy coat.

Meanwhile, Courtney Love was a bit elusive herself. After spending some time in Los Angeles promoting Hole's soon-to-be-released album, entitled 'Live Through This', she cancelled the very first date of her U.K. tour on April 4. Her management offered the explanation that she needed to "focus on the greater good — the health and happiness of her immediate family."

Tragically, some time the very next day Kurt Cobain shot himself; his body was not to be found for three days.

The day before it was discovered that her husband was dead, Courtney Love summoned a doctor to her hotel room for herself, claiming she was undergoing an allergic reaction to prescription drugs. She was arrested upon release from hospital later that day under charges of drug, drug paraphernalia and stolen property possession. It was put forth that she had come near to a heroin overdose in her hotel room. Her lawyer denied all charges; she was released on $10,000 bail.

The press speculated as to the whereabouts of Frances Bean during this time of upheaval, although it was later confirmed that the eighteen-month-old baby was safe and sound at her mother's family home.

On the morning of April 8, 1994, an electrician arrived at the Cobain home in Seattle and spotted what he thought was a mannequin lying on the floor of a small cottage/greenhouse above the garage. Upon closer examination, he realised that what he saw was the body of a young male with a shotgun on his chest. The police arrived and the body, dressed in jeans, a shirt and Converse trainers, was removed for identification. Fingerprints confirmed that it was indeed Kurt Cobain; he was the fourth member of the Cobain family to commit suicide.

Alongside Cobain's body was an identification card and a lengthy note penned in red ink. In this farewell letter Nirvana's lead singer attempted to explain his desperate unhappiness with the band's success, saying, "I haven't felt the excitement of listening to as well as creating music along with reading and writing for too many years now. I feel guilty beyond

"THE WORST CRIME I CAN THINK OF WOULD BE TO PUT PEOPLE OFF BY FAKING IT AND PRETENDING I'M HAVING 100% FUN."
KURT

words for these things . . . the fact is, I can't fool you. Any one of you. It simply isn't fair to you or me. The worst crime I can think of would be to put people off by pretending as if I'm having 100% fun. Sometimes I feel as if I should have a punch-in time clock before I walk out on stage. I've tried everything within my power to appreciate it and I do, God believe me I do, but it's not enough."

Moving on to address his family, he says, "I have a goddess of a wife who sweats ambition and empathy . . . and a daughter who reminds me too much of what I used to be. Full of love and joy, kissing every person she meets because everyone is good and will do her no harm. And that terrifies me to the point to where I can barely function. I can't stand the thought of Frances becoming the miserable, self destructive death rocker that I've become."

His final written words were "Thank you all from the pit of my burning nauseous stomach for your letters and concern during the past years. I'm too much of an erratic, moody person. I don't have the passion anymore and so remember, it's better to burn out than to fade away."

The pain, anguish and sorrow felt by Kurt Cobain's family and friends at the loss of his life cannot be documented. The events immediately following his death give an indication of the grief his fans underwent. While 200 close friends and immediate family gathered at the Holy Unity Church of Truth in Seattle on the evening of April 9, a public ceremony took place at the Seattle Flag Pavilion. Over 5,000 fans held a candlelight vigil in memory of the musical talent whom they had regarded as their spokesperson and whose songs had affected their lives. A tape recording of Courtney Love reading the suicide note her husband had left behind was played over loudspeakers to the crowd. Love would later appear at the gathering in person, clutching a lock of her late husband's hair.

The influence of Nirvana will be felt for many years to come. At once seminal and representative of a generation's angst, Nirvana had captured common feelings of despair, frustration and confusion and transformed them into music unlike any heard before. Kurt Cobain's memory remains strong within the music community. Chris Novoselic, Dave Grohl and Courtney Love continue their musical careers. Frances Bean Cobain will grow up without her father. As Courtney Love cried in response to her husband's contention that to fake his enjoyment of music was a crime, "No! The worst crime is leaving."

NIRVANA
SELECTED DISCOGRAPHY

SUB POP SINGLES

Love Buzz / Big Cheese
1988: Sub Pop SP 23 (1,000 copies)

Sliver / Dive
1990: Sub Pop SP 72 (3,000 copies)

Molly's Lips / Candy – by Fluid
1991: Sub Pop SP 97 (7,500 copies)

ALBUMS

BLEACH

Blew / Floyd The Barber / About A Girl / School / Love Buzz / Paper Cuts / Negative Creep / Scoff / Swap Meet / Mr. Moustache / Sifting / Big Cheese / Downer

UK - 1989: Tupelo TUP LP6
(original release: 2,300 copies)

UK - 1989: Tupelo TUP CD6 (re-release)

UK - 1992: Geffen GEFD 24433 (re-release)

US - 1989: Sub Pop SP 34b

NEVERMIND

Smells Like Teen Spirit / In Bloom / Come As You Are / Breed / Lithium / Polly / Territorial Pissings / Drain You / Lounge Act / Stay Away / On A Plain / Something In The Way / bonus track (not listed): Endless, Nameless
1991: Geffen DGCD 24425

INCESTICIDE

Dive / Sliver / Stain / Been A Son / Turnaround / Molly's Lips / Son Of A Gun / (New Wave) Polly / Beeswax / Downer / Mexican Seafood / Hairspray Queen / Aero Zeppelin / Big Long Now / Aneurysm
1992: Geffen DGCD 24504

IN UTERO

Serve The Servants / Scentless Apprentice / Heart-Shaped Box / Rape Me / Frances Farmer Will Have Her Revenge On Seattle / Dumb / Very Ape / Milk It / Pennyroyal Tea / Radio Friendly Unit Shifter / Tourette's / All Apologies
1993: Geffen DGCD 24607

UNPLUGGED IN NEW YORK

About A Girl / Come As You Are / Jesus Doesn't Want Me For A Sunbeam / The Man Who Sold The World / Pennyroyal Tea / Dumb / Polly / On A Plain / Something In The Way / Plateau / Oh Me / Lake Of Fire / All Apologies / Where Did You Sleep Last Night
1994: Geffen DGCD 24727